Routledge Revivals

Inside the Underworld

First published in 1972, *Inside the Underworld* gives a general picture of the underworld, showing it as it really is, stripped of romanticism and popular misconceptions—a non-stop resistance movement against the forces of law and order, whose ranks include both the weak and the strong, the skilled and the bungling.

How do robbers, con-men, and heisters function? What makes a top gang? Is underworld society different from ordinary society? What kind of clubs do criminals frequent? What is their taste in clothes, in girls, in jokes? Is the modern criminal most at home in Mayfair, Cannes, or Soho? What happens to his wife, his girls, his family when he goes to prison? Can he get policemen to take bribes or turn a blind eye to flagrant crimes? Questions such as these are answered as Peta Fordham unfolds her panorama of the underworld, and the reader will be able to learn many of the humdrum, sad and funny facts of life on the wrong side of the law. The author introduces an amazing variety of underworld characters, refugees from 'straight society' as well as callous and compulsive villains. Among her vignettes is the story of the young man who was largely responsible for changing the nature of British criminal expertise.

Mrs Fordham shows in considerable detail the changing attitudes of the underworld to the law, the police, to violence, and to international gangsterism.

Inside the Underworld

Peta Fordham

Routledge
Taylor & Francis Group

First published in 1972
by George Allen & Unwin Ltd

This edition first published in 2025 by Routledge
4 Park Square, Milton Park, Abingdon, Oxon, OX14 4RN

and by Routledge
605 Third Avenue, New York, NY 10017

Routledge is an imprint of the Taylor & Francis Group, an informa business

Publisher's Note
The publisher has gone to great lengths to ensure the quality of this reprint but points out that some imperfections in the original copies may be apparent.

Disclaimer
The publisher has made every effort to trace copyright holders and welcomes correspondence from those they have been unable to contact.

A Library of Congress record exists under LCCN: 72197393

ISBN: 978-1-041-06395-7 (hbk)
ISBN: 978-1-003-63523-9 (ebk)
ISBN: 978-1-041-06397-1 (pbk)

Book DOI 10.4324/9781003635239

INSIDE THE UNDERWORLD

by Peta Fordham

London · George Allen & Unwin Ltd
RUSKIN HOUSE MUSEUM STREET

First published in 1972

ISBN 0 04 364006 0

Printed in Great Britain
in 11 point Baskerville type
by Clarke, Doble & Brendon Ltd
Plymouth

For my friends,
J. T. T., also known as 'The Guv'
without whom this book could not have been written,
and Dolores
who did not live to see the book for which she waited

Acknowledgements

A great many people have helped me with this book. Unfortunately, I cannot thank most of them openly but they know how grateful I am. My thanks are also due to the Editor of the *Spectator*, who has most generously allowed me to make use (slightly altered) of material published there relating to the McKay case. Some of the material relating to Tommy has also appeared before, in the old *Queen Magazine* and, although no question of copyright arises here, I should still like to thank its successor, *Harper's-Queen*, for being generally helpful.

As always, I owe a deep debt of wifely gratitude. Not many Queen's Counsel would put up with the difficulties my activities present at times. For help, support and encouragement, I say heartfelt thanks – for disturbed nights and a much occupied telephone, I apologise, knowing that I shall be forgiven.

Contents

Introduction

INITIATION INTO THE UNDERWORLD

The village in which I was brought up presented the child with an ordered pattern of life. Each man had his place in it: God had 'made them, high and lowly, and ordered their estate'. The butcher was Mr Blake, Mr Odgers was the greengrocer, old Miss Linnell had the sweetshop and Mrs Bates sold tripe. The Church had an estate of its own which embraced the vicar, the curate, another Mr Blake (the verger) and Mr Wicks the grave-digger. There was also a family named Smith, whose father was often absent but who, on reappearance from prison, was generally to be found doing odd jobs for the vicar. This was Mr Smith the burglar and I came early to the conclusion that burgling was *his* estate. Thus does early conditioning begin.

Mr Smith developed into a faithful client of my father, who had been called to the Bar at about the time of my birth and who was a conscientious and kindly man, a 'soft touch' for the hard-luck story and someone who was genuinely distressed by the fate which overtook the families of men sent to prison. This fate, in the absence of other help, meant the workhouse, an institution which had, in my childhood, scarcely altered since the days of Dickens. My mother had a morbid dread of infectious disease, so intense that our nurse was always told to cross the road if the pram encountered a 'poor' child and to shun the whole street if she perceived the 'fever-cart' – the van which collected linen for disinfection. Duty however was duty. We were made to trot alongside my mother on the weekly call upon the families of clients unfortunate enough to be at the receiving-end of the Poor Law.

The workhouse took no chances of immoral conduct, though our Fallen Woman (an estate I forgot to mention) did actually get pregnant twice there, producing, on the second occasion, beautiful twins who were christened Mary and Joseph, in deference to the holy nuns who at that point decided to take her into their care. Pregnancy was beyond my ken; and when the Fallen Woman, in answer to my questioning about the origin of the twins, informed me that they had been made on the stairs, miraculous conception assumed a meaning for me that it has never had again!

But in the workhouse, the sexes were segregated. I can still see the sad faces of the old ladies, unable to talk to their husbands of a lifetime save through the bars which separated the two compounds, like prisoners in a concentration camp. We plied them with limited consolation on our visits – strong peppermints for the old wives and a twist of shag tobacco for the men. Even a five-year-old could sense that something was wrong here; no doubt I also heard, without quite taking it in, scraps of grown-up criticism.

Our criminal families were allowed to remain with their mother if they were small; but other grim places awaited any child within hailing distance of puberty, a dangerous condition which often led to something called 'The Reformatory', whose scholars had the whole gallery on one side of the church reserved for them. The position was ideal for the propulsion of pellets and anything handy during Morning Service. Some were already delinquents, some I think merely came from 'bad' homes. 'Good' children admired their reckless daring.

Times were economical. Sailor suits were handed down to me from my brother's wardrobe, a kilted skirt being substituted for trousers; and eventually these worn out garments would take on yet another life upon the little Smiths, who were told to express gratitude but who looked just about as grateful as I should have been in the circumstances. Their slum neighbours must have found this fancy dress amusing.

Introduction to underworld families was not, as it happened, via the Smiths, though they were later to play quite a part in my life. The first encounter took place in my mother's absence or it would probably never have occurred at all. I was playing with a top one afternoon, outside my father's study where a patch of stone provided a good base, when I saw within a weeping woman, accompanied by a sharp-faced, grubby little boy, whose constant interruptions were being punctuated at regular intervals by a swipe from his mother, a yelp from the child and an immediate return to the *status quo*.

My father, who looked harassed as well he might, caught sight of me and opened the window. He suggested that I should take the little boy, Billy by name, to see the rabbits. 'Me dad's in trouble', said Billy in explanation. The doings of adults did not particularly interest me and I should probably have had little recollection of this particular meeting, had it not been for the fact that Billy had ringworm, which he duly transferred to me, a happening which confirmed my mother's worst fears. Billy did not live far away and he was friends with Freddie Smith: with hindsight I imagine their fathers 'worked' together. Freddie and Lily Smith were well known to us, as was Daisy the little sister who was 'soft'; and Freddie, who was later to become unpleasantly notorious, was a boon, though forbidden companion, especially when hay-making time left us in the charge of old Henry (rather than Nanny) – a custodian from whom we instantly played truant. Our village was still in the country and we wandered safely at will. Freddie had exciting experience to offer. He knew the local gypsy children whose stealing was professional and skilful and whose nature lore was profound. To this day I owe them a debt for much information.

My father was a popular Counsel as a defender of the Smith friends (almost always hopeless cases) and the circle of children we knew from sorrowful visits expanded. Not unnaturally – especially after the ringworm happening – I was forbidden to consort with them in any way, save *de haut en bas*; and I did not in fact see much of them at this stage, except for Freddie, with whom I constantly squabbled for leadership of a select gang. When I began to go to school in Birmingham, five miles away, I discovered, however, that there were a lot of familiar faces around.

The swimming baths which we patronised (only on Thursdays – clean water day) lay in an unsalubrious area surrounded by the back-to-back houses still to be seen in Birmingham, though television aerials now sprout above them and tenants' cars are parked in the streets. These houses were then filthy, verminous and mostly without sanitation, save for a joint pump and privy in the centre of each square. There was a veto on using the road which ran through them both by school and parents, a longer one being available which used the main streets: the whole area had, even during my mother's life time, been one which the police had only dared to enter in couples or more and where the military had had to be called in to clear the site for redevelopment of the main street. This fact might be remembered when speaking of violence today: it is not so long ago that whole areas of our cities were as unsafe as New York now is. But the more enterprising of us naturally took the forbidden short cut and there, growing in knowledge and in general vice, were the Smiths and others, friendliness itself, calling Ma out to see us and sometimes Pa, shirt-sleeved, moustached and capped or occasionally bowler-hatted; usually drunk and very happy to shake hands with the daughter of his soft-hearted 'brief'. This was all forbidden fruit; but so was almost everything else in those days and I was hungry, for it was war-time. Ma Smith was a rare hand with faggots,[1] when the family was in the money, and I was soon introduced to the delights of chitterlings[2] and other unspeakable delicacies – all to my famished palate delicious.

At this stage, never given pocket money, I also stole small sums regularly from my mother, to the admiration of Freddie and Lily whose Ma would have 'skelped' them had they tried it on with her. My mother never found out: it enabled me to exchange gifts – lime tablets of viridian green or Packer's chocolate (four ounces a penny and extremely soapy) and thereby keep face with my acquaintances. I had taken the first steps to delinquency.

It became apparent in the course of time, however, that crime was neither a satisfactory nor a normal way of making a living and that the criminal's life was a rotten one to live. But this was not until I had begun to know something about it and to hear a great deal more. In the meantime, I acquired (legally) a

[1] **Faggots: a great Midland delicacy made from the 'pluck' of pigs.**
[2] **Chitterlings: pigs' bowels, I believe!**

bicycle and increased liberty. In the parks Freddie's gang were generally mooching around and, as we fed captive animals or, in adjacent gardens, stole fruit or wrote rude words on young marrows, I was unconsciously absorbing their outlook. They had the cunning of young foxes. It is a miracle that I never got into trouble, for they would certainly have deserted me and their evasive tactics were much superior to mine.

During my teens, my father got the idea that I had some interest in his clients and encouraged me to pursue acquaintance, though this scarcely developed in the manner he envisaged. Several children, some later to come to various bad ends, also got lumbered with me as godmother. By now there were a number of criminal homes where I was virtually wallpaper and, at this stage, I suppose I must have heard things which related to 'jobs' in the offing – something that never happens now. The underworld is full of suspicion: it is also full of over-confidence. Since I never split on them (partly at least because to do so would have involved me) I became trusted; and trusted I have, I think, remained through succeeding generations: to acquire the strange position of being confidante without condoning their actions. Nowadays I take great care not to know what I should not at the wrong moment – not difficult, since one is rarely told in advance anything that matters. Trust and confidence are also relative: suspicion is easily if temporarily aroused. I am by no means universally beloved; but they mostly return when they are in trouble.

It was many years before any one in my own world, save my husband, took the slightest interest in my other one. Not until I wrote *The Robbers' Tale* (which is the accurate inside story of the Great Mail Train Robbery) did Fleet Street discover that I had led, as it were, a double life. The years between childhood and the present day had been filled with jobs that were almost always concerned with factual information of some sort, because that is my kind of journalism: the War kept me more on foreign than home affairs but always, not very far in the background, were the contacts, the disturbed nights, the tragi-comedies and the human nature in the raw which have been close to me all my life from the 'other side of the fence'. War-time produced some interesting reactions from the underworld. Patriotism and graft, self-interest and a great longing to be called upon to open enemy safes or give other professional assistance, real courage and a lot of cowardice and desertion all mingled. I was still an ear: if I did nothing else for my country, at least I have listened to people who, like King Midas, had an absolute compulsion to tell someone about official secrets of this kind. There were not many recruits from the underworld to Intelligence; but many, many envious eyes were cast.

I had always free-lanced on a number of subjects and have continued to do so, but after my book was published, I spent six happy years with *The Sunday Times*, with the somewhat equivocal title of 'crime consultant'. We had some splendid stories together; but I think my underworld acquaintances were relieved when this came to an end. They don't trust journalists and I was always aware that the old confidence was watered down with a fear that 'my paper' might somehow manage to twist my elbow. There is something altogether more satisfactory about being professionally detached, so as to pursue with greater freedom things that one really cares about.

Some of these will be apparent in my book. Views are rightly liable to criticism: what I should like, however, to disarm in advance, is exasperation on the part of the reader that there is a degree of repetition and a frequent taking up of certain aspects of criminal life or activity in different chapters. No one is more aware of this than I am; but the underworld is not a subject which divides itself neatly into sections and such topics as, say, violence and corruption, keep on cropping up in slightly different context. One can speak of the general view of a group of criminals, only to have to deal with the whole thing over again when it reappears somewhere else with a variation. So I ask for forbearance and for the realisation that the underworld is the most untidy society that it is possible to find.

These personal details have been included because the first question everyone asks me is how I became involved with the underworld and the answer supplies some of my credentials for writing a book of this sort. I suppose my real qualification is that of being able to see people of another culture in relaxed and entirely natural surroundings – something that no person connected with 'authority' ever does. The situation is often a tricky one but it is fair to say that they know, as well as I do, that my husband's professional position has to be safe-guarded and that I cannot therefore be so relaxed; but, born and bred in the law, it is second nature to me to listen and accept 'the client's' story (even if I do not believe it) and to respect professional confidences.

In the course of the years there have been dark and terrible moments, but there has also been a lot of comedy. I have not taken sides. One of my oldest underworld friends who passed various passages for publication said to me indignantly, 'Whose side are you on?', and was not at all happy with my reply 'Nobody's'. If anything constructive can be done about crime the first thing to understand is what makes criminals tick. I have tried to depict the underworld as it really is and perhaps a well-known (but none the less true) legal anecdote illustrates what this means. It fell to a nervous and inexperienced young Counsel to address a particularly difficult Judge on behalf of an equally difficult client. 'My Lord', said the young barrister, after all too short a speech, 'There isn't anything else I can say. This may not be a defence; but perhaps it is *some* explanation of my client's actions.' I cannot better his hope.

Chapter 1

A LOOKING-GLASS WORLD

'There is not an honourable man or an honest woman
among them – but all is human.'
John Gay, *The Beggar's Opera*, 1728

No one has ever drawn a picture of the underworld as accurately as did John Gay. He knew well the *braggadacio*, fatalism, snobbery and vitality that exist there. Its essentials are still what they were in his time, and if it were possible to transpose, by some time-machine, a modern professional criminal back into the eighteenth-century London of *The Beggar's Opera*, he would find his way about confidently in a couple of days, recognizing familiar attitudes and codes, discovering the same comradeship and treacheries and, in the main, finding that thread of continuity which has run through the centuries in this murky yet compelling world.

To the outsider, the frontiers of the underworld are no longer as sharply defined as they were in Gay's day or, for that matter, as they were even a quarter of a century ago. Its inhabitants are not recognisable on sight any more. A member can still recognise another (indeed nearly everyone knows everyone else), but the chance visitor from outside does not often spot the villain[1] these days unless he is given some clue. I do not think 'Michael' who appears in the next chapter would have been recognised even as a beginner in crime. Times and the social scene have changed, if the underworld itself has not altered in basic essentials.

To be a 'criminal', i.e. a convicted person, does not necessarily admit you to the underworld itself. A recent television series began by the attempt to define exactly what is meant by a criminal – a

[1] 'Villain', which sounds almost a 'jokey' word is, in fact, the normal name for a professional criminal as used by the criminals themselves and the police. The latter seldom use any other word.

difficult enough task. It is even harder to trace out membership of the underworld. Even those shady characters who fiddle and cheat most of the time are not considered as fellow members by the underworld without some further involvement. You enter the underworld almost as you become admitted to one of the City Livery Companies of London – by patrimony or by invitation. Sometimes you are welcomed because it is clear that you have qualified or because in 'someone's' opinion, you are likely material. 'Someone' is a great underworld word. Its anonymity is often used when information is being sought, to suggest that wild horses could not drag the name out of the teller of the tale: as the evening wears on, the name usually emerges, but honour has been satisfied. Once admitted, you are, like the Livery man, 'free' of a community which consists of overlapping social circles, some more exclusive than others. One of the realities of life there is that almost everyone suspects everyone else all the time, but the binding force is that all are part of a non-stop resistance movement against the society which is based on law and order. Once inside the member will speak of himself and other members as 'we': 'they' are both the enemy and the means of livelihood, for the underworld lives on them and is sent to prison by them. Life will become a continuous attempt to outwit the 'Law', which means the police, not the Statute Book. The war that will be waged on society will be a series of skirmishes and many defeats will be expected but some victories too. This will be accepted, even if colleagues are basically rather stupid, as most of one's underworld companions will be. There will be enjoyment in the 'kicks', for there will be plenty of adventure, albeit often of a squalid kind.

Good qualities do exist there, but values are reversed. The loving husband takes incredible risks to steal a fancied piece of jewellery for his wife, as a proof of his affection; loyalty among friends is founded on joint knavery and cemented both by criminal activity and adversity; comradeship which would be the making of a Commando unit flashes into life on a major robbery: men have (occasionally!) been known to accept a long term of imprisonment rather than betray a friend. G. K. Chesterton, who was always fascinated by the mind of the wrong-doer, once remarked that the word 'good' had many meanings. I think the definition was something like this: 'As for instance, if a man shot his grandmother at a mile away, you would say of him that he was a good shot, but not necessarily a good man.' I have tried this one on several underworld characters and not one, so far, has thought it funny; which suggests an interesting mental block.

Chesterton was right: the 'good' job, the 'real' mate, even the well-known euphemism of 'straightening' which means, of course, making crooked, are evidence of the reversal of meaning in this world. In all seriousness, one of the older generation frequently describes friends of his as 'little angels' – and means it: their strings of convictions (one six-footer angel is a violent detainee in a top-security wing at the moment) have no meaning for him. In K's world, they conform to the proper standard. 'An absolutely trustworthy driver' friend of his obliged me with a lift home recently. He was Tony, a trusted 'stoppo', an escape driver. There was no hurry but he cut through traffic at top speed, took a short cut down a one-way against the flow, and went round several roundabouts the wrong way, just to show professional skill. Yet he was, by their standards, trustworthy. If the respectable cab-driver were as punctual as Tony he would never be late on a job, never fail to turn up. But Tony is not a taxi-driver: he is the man waiting round the corner who drives in to pick up the thieves at the door of the cleaned-out premises, whisking them away before the Law can give chase. Viewed objectively, liable to knock down and perhaps kill (unintentionally) and drive on (intentionally) on the job, he is a dangerous man leading a criminal life. To begin to understand the way Tony ticks, one must shed ordinary codes and accept, so far as the underworld is concerned, the ethics of their surroundings. As in that well-known newspaper, 'All human life is there'; and the honest observer will often stop appalled, as he sees, in the distorting mirror, something uncomfortably close to his own reflection; but one cannot moralise whilst observing.

It is basically this recognition by the others and the acceptance of the community code that marks the underworld member. To say where recruits come from is not always easy. Crime is, in the first place, a persistently hereditary thing. Many criminals have a genealogical table going back many generations. Recruitment, either from boys too stupid to do anything but drift into crime or from others, less stupid, who just get into mischief and stay in it from deliberate choice, is always easy. The former become a pool of employable dishonest labour and are eventually to be found as the recidivist inmates of our prisons. Brighter boys – the only ones who are likely to be salvageable and that rarely – can work upwards in the hierarchy. They have often quite genuine social ambitions, seeing crime originally as a quick means to make money: they are the ones who tend to bring in recruits of a higher social class, perhaps with technical know-how or special knowledge which helps with 'fencing'. Sometimes it is possible to observe a rivalry in the ranks akin to that which can be seen in Whitehall between established and unestablished personnel. But the steady core of the underworld has for long been born into it, and there never seems to be any difficulty with recruitment. There are countless criminal families and they move about. The grandchildren of the Birmingham underworld whom I knew in childhood are, for instance, doing well in London, Manchester and Liverpool today. It does not always run in the straight descent but somewhere along the line there will be a relative who is 'well respected' – another great underworld term of approbation. There is no criminal recommendation more valued than legend which has grown about a previous generation though, as in the respectable world, it is youth who is the god these days, and one is described as 'past it' by middle age! The rising young crook speaks with disdain of a 35-year-old, but I have observed no reluctance to consult the veteran. A well-respected haunt of well-respected crooks continually brings into contrast the differences and the resemblances between the older generation and the new and is worth a long, cool look.

The club in question – the Badger's Club – is not easily discovered by the idly curious. Its present location, as usual, is close to London's most exclusive clubs. Like its prestigious rivals, the door bears no sign of its existence: its telephone number, though the actual instrument must be red-hot at such times as when the 3 o'clock race results are coming through, remains ex-directory.

Inside, though it is licensed neither for drink nor gambling, it has some of the best drink in London and few places see card-playing later at night or gambling for higher stakes. It is a peaceful place as a rule: there are exceptions, tiresome ones, disliked by all since a serious row can involve a change of site. The club has been in existence a long time and is greatly valued by its members as a centre of information and, at times, as a source of comfort and succour.

This membership is carefully vetted. Familiar faces are naturally absent for varying periods, but are always welcomed back without nosey questions. Curiosity about personal matters is a breach of underworld manners. Not even the Athenaeum has stricter rules, though here they are found in no book. There is no annual meeting; for the club, as a registered club, has no existence. It is merely there; and, if blackballing is thereby made difficult and blackmail sometimes wins admission, a firm internal ostracism of unpopular people mostly maintains membership and visitors as the club prefers things to be. Class distinction may be disappearing in the outside world, but not here. Women may, in the outside world, have encroached upon male preserves. They seldom cross the threshold here; and, if they are admitted, upon sufferance, they realise their place, strictly below the salt. They must not even ring their husbands up, except in dire emergency, and must never use a name when they do so. In fact, of course, few wives even know the telephone number. If they are entrusted with it, they will know what code to use.

To obtain admittance is difficult. Unless an enquirer is prepared to forsake his ordinary vocation and take to the underworld, he is unlikely to gain entry, though from time to time, a trusted guest accompanies a member on a visit. For the Badger's historic premises (the continuity is in membership, not accommodation) house what is probably the most faithful lineal descendant of the centuries-old 'thieves' kitchen' and the present name is the nickname of its proprietor, a redoubtable veteran. But Badger's has moved with the times. I wish that the understandable anonymity and publicity-shunning of the underworld were not so tight. The club is a living documentary of the underworld: if only there had been club photographs, year after year! In the old days, when the race-gangs lorded it around, a thief looked like a thief: the face of violence then was what the insurance advertisements like us to believe it looks like now. Life has got softer for us all, despite ulcers (burglars have them too, usually from wife-trouble); and the underworld likes its comforts these days. The membership, in the old days, looked a depressed class. This was not surprising. They were. They had to work harder to keep body, soul and family together, and it was the heyday of private enterprise, when a man – or a thief – had to rely on himself and his own endeavours to earn his bread. A villain looked old at thirty: he was really past it at fifty.

What is more, there was no National Assistance. So, when the breadwinner was convicted, the wife and children were liable to be on the rates, which, in sterner times, meant the workhouse in conditions of Dickensian squalor which are forgotten today. Few have a keener sense of their rights than wrongdoers and nowadays, if ready cash is short, the grass-widows make no bones about it. They are round to the Social Security at once. But, since crime has been upgraded too and its wages are more profitable, a wife who is content to work whilst her man is in prison usually manages, what with the Children's Allowances and the like, to get by; though it is still a matter of hardship for less well-found wives to travel long distances on prison visits. As in the rest of society things are also more permissive: wives can now have boyfriends whilst the husband is away, provided always that they do not touch 'the money'. That way lies violence and many an unexplained tragedy.

If the old-time membership looked more harassed and older, older in fact it often was, for the age of delinquency has fallen with earlier maturity and top thieves are young today. The most striking difference is in dress and general appearance. The 'old school' boys would never have dreamt of going into West End hotels except to rob: indeed, they would not have got past the porter. They did not travel abroad and they had no wish to do so. They were not smartly dressed: some were not even very clean of shirt and ties were not inevitable. Cloth caps were usual: in short, the average criminal looked what he was – a working-class man in a class-defined world. There were always some dandies but these were the exception, usually earning themselves derisive nicknames which bespoke their fanciful ideas. The old hands were, in their own way, honest craftsmen, which is to say, in ours, thunderingly dishonest; but at least they worked hard; and they kept themselves much more to themselves.

Things are very different today, for the underworld, as ever, reflects clearly the progress of the respectable one, albeit always some way behind in its manners and customs. If the voices in the Badger's today are not Establishment in intonation, the appearance of the membership is well up to that of any good club frequented by men about town. The accent is on good, sharp but by no means over-trendy dressing. They go to the best tailors; not the best-known, because it is a little awkward to ask a Savile Row tailor to make up a lovely lot of cloth from a stolen bolt; so it has to be a craftsman who knows both his business and his customer. Shirts are whiter than white and clothes look as if they lived at the expensive cleaners. Probably they do – on unpaid accounts. (It is a regrettable fact that Counsel in court often look scruffy and even grubby by comparison with their clients.)

All still look older than their real age, though they no longer look a depressed class: on the contrary, they look uncommonly prosperous. People of this sub-culture do not, on the whole, make old bones. The pursuit of ill-gotten gains, whether by financier or thief, must be full of stress: I made myself very unpopular by saying this a short time ago on a visit to one of the prisons. The hardships of this particular nick on appearance had been extremely rejuvenating and no one could ascribe it to an ideal diet.

To understand changes in the Badger's Club, one has to look at the way in which crime is and was done. Suppose we take a not entirely mythical Fred, aged sixty, and compare his criminal activities with those of young Fred, his last-born pride and his occasional joy.

Old Fred was born in an Islington slum, and at an early age concluded that a God-fearing mother's ideas of a heavenly crown for him were less capable of realisation than the immediate proceeds of theft. He started by stealing bicycles with the 'bad' boys of the neighbourhood; was eventually caught and, on the second occasion, sentenced to three months. In the nick, where he felt lonely and frightened, he struck up a friendship with another, brighter boy, who was a much more expert thief. What followed – and this is not mythical at all – was a lifetime of devoted partnership, comradeship of a high order and non-stop criminal enterprise. The two of them collected a small circle of friends, upon whose talents they could draw; and settled down to what is known as professional 'screwing'. This term does not have the same meaning in the underworld as it does with the respectable: the underworld is a great deal more prudish and it simply means stealing.

In and out of prison they went. A good job meant hard work. First they had to work out where to go. Then to 'case the joint'. A country house could involve many a damp night in shrubberies, a lot of hanging about in the local, making a beer last a long time because you were working, not boozing. The habits of servants when left in charge had to be known and calculated. Sometimes, they had to be seduced – in the way of business only. If it was a jewel job, all this work might go for nothing. On the chosen night, when everything seemed settled, the lady of the house would suddenly have made up her mind to wear to a dinner party the one diamond piece that the maid had assured everyone she never used except in London. Safes that had been guaranteed 'pieces of cake' failed to respond to professional coaxing. 'I remember', said one veteran crook, 'how we had worked for months on a country house, where there was a nice little safe, as easy as easy, the butler said. Well, come the night we'd arranged, everything went right till we started on the lock. "A piece of cake!" I said to my mate, "this is going to take hours and if we jell it, the noise is sure to wake the maids." Then I have an idea. There's a ladder outside so we get it in and ease the safe out of its bed in the wall (and that's tough work I can tell you) and we get it on the ladder so as to put it in the van – luckily the job's a ground-floor one. We've only got it through the window when the ladder snaps and the safe goes on the flags with a bang – so we scarper and wait. But nothing moves so we come back again and use the half. This time we get it to the drive when the blasted thing goes again and now there's a light goes on in the house. So we have to quit. Heartbreaking really, isn't it – after all the work we put in!'

Nor were town jobs exactly easy. There was always a risk of being caught with a marked *Kelly's Directory* in the car – a risk which exists today. It is an education to walk through Mayfair or Belgravia with one of the old boys and to plumb his knowledge of house tenants and exactly which premises are still interesting to him. Even the precaution of getting a pal into the job of faithful butler, trusted with all the keys, always left the possibility that the law might have noticed the other pal in the getaway car. These were no Jaguar jobs. A bull-nosed Morris was about the mark in those days and the speed with which crimes were set up was correspondingly slow. They say that a simple good jewel robbery could take anything from two months to six or seven to organise in those days, even if you had all the luck you wanted; and meantime you had to live. Afterwards there was the fencing – and fences are hard businessmen. Victims too can be unpredictable. One dogged operator told me that years ago he made great plans to rob a well-known comedy actress. I thought it a very funny story but the teller did not. He was merely indignant. 'I got under her bed', he said, 'I knew the time she came in and I made a little slit in the hangings. Well, like I said, in she comes, throws everything down, including the rocks, and she's in bed in two shakes. The wife told me she'd be hours doing her face, but not a bit of it. I don't think she even washed. So I think it'll only be a few minutes now and I'm reckoning up what the fence'll pay me when suddenly – on goes the light. 'Course I think she's spotted me and I'm fair sweating but not a bit of it! She nips out of bed and the next thing I see through the slit is her, looking at herself in the mirror from bed, with a dirty great hat on her head. And d'you know, she starts reading a part! For over two hours she keeps it up, till I'm fair dropping. Oh! I could have done 'er and no kidding. It's past three when she turns the light out and I'm that done, I can't even bother with the rocks. Anyway I reckoned she was an unlucky touch. Come to think of it, I've never had any luck with show-biz.' So there *was* truth in Nanny's stories about burglars under beds! This particular operator was a great hand at hiding in hotel bedrooms, especially in thick curtains. I doubt if anyone does it today.

Young Fred, who does not like his name and uses others such as Keith or Terry, looks quite different from his father. He dresses with confidence and goes as near being trendy as is wise. It does not do to stand out too much in surroundings where you do not wish to attract notice, and he is sensible enough to know this. He has had a much better education than his father: not that he paid much attention to it at the time but he picked up odd scraps and, being an intelligent type (by the standards of his world), used what he had amassed. Like other ambitious underworld boys, he took care to acquire a 'legit' business, almost inevitably general dealer. This is the classy term for rag and bone merchant plus; and, much more important, is a splendid excuse for having all sorts of stuff on the premises and provides a reason for being in any part of the Home Counties at odd times.

Fred does not 'go' for close friends. He trusts nobody and rather despises his father (though fond of him) for being 'uneducated', out of date, and unambitious. Education is much revered in his circles, though not exactly pursued in them. The idea of spending your whole working life with someone like Uncle John (no relative, just his father's crook partner of a lifetime) strikes him as so old hat he has difficulty about being civil to his father on the subject. Fred means to go for the big stuff. At twenty-two, he has just about emerged from the apprenticeship stage, doing odd jobs for the big boys: earning his spurs as a strong-arm man in some of the clubs, collecting 'rents' on small protection rackets and, best of all to his way of thinking, after working on preliminary small stuff, he has been on some of the 'set-up' jobs, such as lorry hi-jacking, where he has made a very fair wage. On all this, he has proved a trustworthy companion so far. Whilst not violent by nature, he has no objection to the coshing of a nightwatchman or lorry driver in the way of business. This shocks old Fred, who regards violence as a mark of professional incompetence. What shocks him even more is young Fred's obvious determination to remain a freelance, a mercenary to be hired at the bidding of any gangster who offers enough. Gangster, by the way, does not mean just a hoodlum, in English parlance. A gangster here means a hirer of labour. A freelance crook today has almost always got an agent: this is the mobster, who, like all agents, has to have a substantial clientele to live. Hence his 'mob' – usually from the same district. A sharp-eyed observer can spot the mobsters, hawking their clients around the pubs and clubs. Once the 'buzz' of a job is on they will be pressing the claims of their respective young Freds as sharply as any theatrical agent. Pub bars tend to empty mysteriously in some districts when strangers appear.

Young Fred has been abroad under another Christian name. He has not yet married and goes through a number of 'birds', another source of worry to his parents. His ambition is quite simple. One day, he thinks, when he is one of the big boys, he will do the super job and vanish to a life of luxury. A number of such will-o'-the-wisp plans exist in the underworld. He is not going to be such a mug as to tie himself down to a friend or wife. When he has the big money, the doors, he reckons, will be open to him. Meanwhile, he has not got the sense to see that an increasing number of convictions for smallish offences are making him a marked man. But what crook ever did? The supreme gamblers of all time, they await the throw of the dice. In Fred's case, he trusts they will flip him up into the top gangster category one day. Ordering the best in the Badger's, he continues to dream of the great job. Meanwhile, he tries to work on the big, infrequent robberies and refuses the diligent, day-to-day work of the older generation.

Old Fred is not a bad chap, according to his somewhat peculiar standards. He is dishonest steadily and professionally but, in his own circle, is reliable. Young Fred, in another walk of life, would be called a cad and a bounder. But he is only reflecting what his social betters are doing. The fact that he is completely amoral (though having a strong business sense, he is probably more careful about laying girls than are his respectable counterparts) does not differ so greatly from the stupid fecklessness of a lot of the younger generation who seem to keep out of delinquency almost by accident. What will make him a real social menace is, paradoxically enough, one of his few real plus points.

He is an exceptionally good boxer. This, in the underworld,

is greatly revered, both for itself and for the fact that good performers often have access to tickets for fights. It leads young Fred straight into the company of the sporting world which, perhaps no great shakes in itself, is also a stepping stone. Sooner or later, he will run into a new phenomenon in our society and one which has had as much influence on changing the face of the underworld as anything else – the social glorification of sensational crime. Lionised, he will almost certainly become a menace to some other youngsters.

Chapter 2

A ROBBERY ON TAPE

The Beggar who speaks the prologue for Gay was articulate. It is not easy to get a connected narrative out of most working criminals today about their working lives, because they are suspicious and will not willingly run the risks of betrayal. They will yarn on about their prowess but are extremely cagey in some respects, often irrational ones. I have no articulate Beggar to speak for the modern underworld. But I have a spokesman. His tale can serve as an introduction from within.

I might have called it a scoop, because it tells how one man really felt about a real crime. But it is tied up with such a tragic sequel that one thinks of it differently. It is the story of an extremely successful raid on a London jeweller, told me in detail by a man who had taken part in it : an educated 'black sheep' who had got into crime, perhaps for 'kicks', perhaps because he found there a sense of belonging that he had failed to find elsewhere. It can be told frankly because the man concerned is dead : he died by his own hand within days of our last meeting, having got himself into complicated trouble with Continental thugs and having, rumour says, been a catspaw in the sabotage of an aircraft whose destruction killed a great many people. He did not name the shop that was robbed, or who his associates were, so that I cannot point the finger at anyone else. He never betrayed a pal, which was in his favour : and his end was almost heroic, for he tried to take on impossible odds and only when failure was complete and utter did he give in. He did, they say, kill when a French friend was shot in the affair which finally brought him down. The reason he talked at this extraordinary length was not far to seek. Like many another man with a burden on his mind, he had to find someone he could trust, who could act as priest, psychiatrist or – as in my case – just an 'ear'. He was nearly finished when I last saw him, an edgy, rather furtive man, very different from the playboy of two years previously. But, like any other underworld character, he cheered up as he talked, reliving the thrills of a successful 'job'. All this was usual enough. What is extraordinary about his story is that, as an educated man who had been welcomed (though cautiously) by the underworld for financial know-how and help when big transfers and Swiss bank accounts were involved, he had integrated so quickly and taken the colour of his surroundings, thinking and reacting like his associates. He was already warped, and although his words are the words of our world, the attitude is truly criminal, and very articulate.

I have altered as little as possible. A lot of it was on tape, which I should never have got from the born-and-bred criminal, who would not risk a voice-identification. There was a lot of vanity in his make-up and I think he wanted me to write his life-story. I also took voluminous notes and have only edited the material to make the story run smoothly, omitting extraneous stuff and, as promised, have regretfully destroyed the tape. He sounds weak, neither a hero nor an anti-hero, and this is typical of the underworld and, I may add, often draws criticism on to the head of a writer who depicts the criminal as he is. There are a lot of inconsistencies. What to look for in search of typical criminal reactions in the way he tells it is the complete amorality of the approach: he is excited by the 'kicks' of the job, but there is curiously little feeling about any human being in it, except that he feels a certain amount of mild comradeship. It is quite clear that no one gives a damn about the fact that a lot of the stuff they were after – and got – was in the form of heirlooms whose theft would bring great unhappiness to those who had lost them. But notice that he *is* concerned for Charlie's boy's physical warmth, though not his future. Notice also that 'Jim' makes great play about what turned out to be an 'easy touch' – one of those sidelights on underworld boasting. Only one thing is lacking – the over-suspiciousness of the crook. If the teller had lived, when he would undoubtedly have been caught out sooner or later (and probably through betrayal by one of his comrades who got jealous) he might have developed the characteristic suspicion of his world. As it was, he remained rather naïve. So do many of them, though in different ways.

His name was not Michael, but it will serve. I was shocked when I heard of his end but not really sad for him. It wouldn't have been any good for him to go on. In the vernacular of the world he had joined, 'His time had come'.

'You may have guessed that I was on the safe-deposit job I told you about. Well, I went missing for a time after that but I got bored, besides my money was being cut off and there was domestic.[1] I'd wanted to get in on another home job : I was sick of Villefranche and the mob there, so when I found a message for me to get in touch with Jim I was quite bucked. It meant I was in and not before I deserved it, I thought. So if you really want to know –

'Well, anyway, I met Jim down at the pub in the Old Kent. I'd seen him once or twice before, and knew him for a good operator, but this time he only nodded casually. The usual crowd was there. He pushed a Scotch over to me and nodded to the barman. Two other chaps, sitting at the back, got up and went through somewhere. Very well-dressed one of them was, I noticed.

'The day's racing was what they were all talking about, and the big fight. We finished our drinks and Jim got up. I followed as if to go to the Gents, but when we were clear of the bar Jim turned into a little room which looked as though it was used as an office. The other two were already there. "Digger", said Jim, indicating the sharp dresser. "And Charlie. This is Mike, sometimes known as Gentleman Mike if you want to make him mad." We laughed. I rather liked the look of them. He locked the door.

'Jim was pretty businesslike. He explained how I came into the act and mentioned that I had been useful before, but this they knew of course. It was manners. The job was a good one and big. He reckoned that it was a six-handed one, needing skilled burners[2] and a couple of stoppo cars. The bell system was first-class and would need the best though we should try our luck with the security personnel first. Charlie had already got somewhere, having got a cousin of his installed as cleaner, with first-class forged refs. Nellie was now regarded as a treasure by

[1] 'Domestic' means wife-trouble.
[2] 'Burners' – oxy-acetylene or thermic-lance operators.

the shop, always willing to oblige, especially with late hours, taking on anyone's work without grumbling and she had the run of the premises. She had made a special feature of doing a bit of overtime on Saturday mornings, when she chatted up the security-man who saw her off the premises. Nellie knew her business, said Jim. Charlie said sourly that she knew her value too.

'The job had been on the books for some time, hence Jim's care not to be seen talking to us all at once, since he was so well known that it would have roused interest and he didn't want any snout putting the Law on a watch. They had been waiting for a character called Dodger to come out of the nick where he had been languishing on a five-stretch. Another character called Slim was due out almost at once and he was the preferred bell-man,[3] though Digger was hopeful that the outside security man was going to come along with us for a sizeable cut. It was a good time to do the shop as lots of stuff was in for storage and re-setting. The bell system really was tough, said Jim, and would have to be silenced bit by bit. Also, the inside security had to be watched. He didn't look like being straightened, and Nellie wasn't at all keen on trying anything funny since she had relied upon legit cleaning in between the jobs that her cousin Charlie wished on her and didn't want to get mixed up.

'I thought she was a stinker when I met her, a real hard-faced bitch, but business is business. The idea was that Jim, Dodger, Slim, Charlie and I were going to be the break-in party. Digger was fixing cars and was in process of trying to rope in one Fred, a chap with a row of generally successful bank jobs to his credit, to come out of retirement and lend a van. Fred was interested but unenthusiastic. "Any more", said Jim, "and we might as well drop the idea. Too many for the carve-up anyway." He didn't really like Digger either but he was well in with his Australian mob and had super contacts.

'Jim was very careful about planning the drops.[4] We reckoned on a lot of heavy, old-fashioned stuff with heavy settings which

[3] 'Bellman' – the man who silences the alarm-system – the 'bells'.

[4] 'Drops' – someone thought safe from police attention, with whom stolen goods can be left till it is considered safe to collect them. A great source of cheating and friction.

would take a lot of breaking-up, so the drops had to be reliable. I was to take a few really hefty diamonds across to Holland, where they had a good fence. We thought we could probably get it set up within six weeks, provided Dodger and Slim kept their heads and didn't get their "bird"[5] extended. Charlie's wife was passing the messages on visits.

'Digger, Charlie and Jim had built up a kind of diary of the regular comings and goings at Casbourne's,[6] particularly at weekends since this would be a Saturday night/Sunday morning job. What we really had to know about was the vital back entrance where we were going to get in. This was a staircase shared by a whole collection of offices. Nellie said that very few people came in on Saturday to any of them. My fancy accent was to be used to ring up, at artistically separated intervals, every office which shared the back entrance with the jewellers – on Saturdays, that is, and find out who was about. I invented a number of ploys, all of which fell flat because no one was there. The lazy bastards had just what we hoped they had – a deep regard for the five-day week.

'I got to know and like Jim a lot during the next few weeks, though he was always cagey with me and never met me in public. After he had got over what he called my la-di-da accent, he treated me as an equal – sometimes. He had been born and bred in the East End, the son of an old grafter and had numerous "uncles". He also worked in the old way although he wasn't more than thirty-five, keeping clear of violence on the whole, and prophesied that there would be a return to this way of life after a period of gangsterism. He was a real and I really did go for him

'They explained to me how to deal with a job where the bell-system might be complicated. "This sort of screwing means planks", said Charlie, poring over the floor plan which he had assembled from our joint efforts. "Planks is what you lay across the floor to work on in case they've got it belled. You wouldn't believe how diabolical some of them are. Slim was nicked once

[5] 'Bird' – often used to describe a girlfriend, here means a prison-sentence. I can't imagine why the same word is applied to both!

[6] 'Casbourne' is one of my own family names, used as being less tiresome than continued 'Xs'. It has no hidden significance.

for leaning over to reach a big rock, left on the bench, and it was a diabolical trap – wired so as he didn't hear a thing but the Law did." So we practised walking on planks, and bloody silly we looked.

'Nellie came up with a brainwave. One of the problems of doing a big job is getting the gear into the premises before the day. You don't want to get nicked in the car with a load of ironmongery on the way to a job, so bottles of gas for the burner and so forth are better on the premises. Nellie, the veteran of a lot of jobs, threw out a broom and some detergent from her store and went and complained to the manager about pilfering, and she got the poor sod to agree to a large steel cabinet in the basement to which she alone had the key. We arranged to get the bottles and burning gear in a couple of nights before the day. Planks haven't been called housebreaking implements yet. Jim was going to drop some, plus paint and brushes, to look like a legit. builder's one. He was a builder in his spare time – very spare. The bottles were going to be knocked off from a building-site near Victoria, where the nightwatchman was a pal. "No need to buy expensive", said Charlie with a grin.

'The boys got out of the nick on schedule. We got down to the last details. These were the silencing of the bells on the back-door of the shop. Nellie had got an impression of the outer door key to the common staircase. The security man was co-operating though windy, and had tipped us off that this door itself was a relatively simple job, only guarded by an ordinary alarm which goes off when the opening of the door breaks the contact between the steel button on its spring in the jamb and the recess into which it fits. What was more important, he had promised that he would be on duty that night and take the fuse out in the headquarters for half an hour, just in case. But Jim didn't rely on him.

'To inactivate this alarm, we had to get the exact height from the floor at which the button was placed, cut out a tiny slit and pass through this a screwdriver which would keep contact whilst Slim bridged the wires which would inactivate the alarm. Once inside and the door closed, all would look okay and undisturbed. We should then proceed section by section. Charlie had a kid, a good little grafter in the making, who was going up on the roof with a walkie-talkie to watch for anything suspicious. George, the driver, was an old hand. The signal for the pickup was a slip of blank paper shoved under the door. George knew how to make himself scarce and yet keep the eye.

'Slim gave us the needle badly by being spotted making a book in the nick at the very last minute, but managed to get away with it – the Governor was soft – and emerged on time. Digger turned up with an unappetising rash on him. He looked like something out of Dickens, and I hoped it wasn't the clap or worse. But he was a likeable guy. What was more, he had picked up an old boy in the nick who had let it slip that he had had a go on the same jewellers twelve years previously, and the old boy told him that there had been in his time a secondary bell system, well hidden, attached to the inner part of the vault. "No warning", said the old grafter, "it was a direct line and the first thing you knew was bogies all over the place." We could check this by looking for high-up wires, as the point of entry had to be visible.

'Jim decided that he had got to look after this warning and wanted Slim to come with him, which Slim, who reckoned he was being watched, was pretty unwilling to do. However, we got a Metropolitan Water Board friend to lend us his gear, so he called at one of the offices above Casbourne's and cooked up a yarn about stopcocks and then got a girl to take him down to Nellie's den, where, whilst the girl made him a cuppa, he poked about a bit and returned with the news that all the wires coming out of Casbourne's could be accounted for. "We'll just have to effing well pray that you're right", said Dodger.

'On the Friday evening George called at Casbourne's just as they were closing and announced that he had brought the lino they had ordered. This was a bit of a surprise to them but they were locking up and gladly agreed that the best thing to do was to leave it in the basement over the weekend and sort it out on the Monday. Nobody wanted to bother with it on Saturday morning. It was duly shoved down whilst Nellie carried on about the mess it made – I will say she was an artist. A duff docket was signed and George departed. As soon as he was gone, Nellie investigated the rolls and removed the bottles and burning equipment neatly packed inside. She had a job getting them into her cupboard and eventually shoved some of them under a heap of papers in the corner. Jim cursed her high and low when he heard this, but nothing came of it.

'We knew that the Law generally made a casual inspection about 10.30 p.m. every night, trying the front door and usually having a look at the back. It was a nice little bit of practice for the youngsters. The security man did not stay on at night: his function was to check that the bells were in order and set. So the ideal time for the break-in was right after the first check and well before any other – which meant about 10.45 p.m. on Saturday.

'I must say the location was a piece of cake. There was a clear view of the main street, down which the Law took its evening walk and you could keep a lookout both ways for Pandas. In the coffee-bar opposite, Slim was to take up his position and observe the Law's progress. At 10.40, George, driving a van – which was to be nicked by arrangement with a respectable Bermondsey tradesman[7] who would report its loss at the right moment – would pass by, carrying a small quantity of groceries on top of any last-minute requirements. If all was clear, Slim would emerge, light a cigarette and pass on to the small courtyard at the rear of the shop. Jim would be with George, who would drop him round the next corner. George then hooked it for three hours, staying on a manned telephone line in Notting Hill, not far away. If all was well, he would then begin to pass at hourly intervals, on the hour, looking for the slip of paper under the front door. After three hours he was to try it half-hourly, but being careful not to be noticed. Should anything go desperately wrong, we intended to use the shop phone but only in real emergency, since it might be linked with trouble. His wife was staying near the phone.

'Charlie's boy was a serious kid, about fifteen. He had an intercom we had rigged up from a small ad. in one of the papers but he was only to use it if he saw Squad cars, in which case he

[7] This would mean that the car was not stolen, if questions were asked on the way.

was to warn us and open the skylight which he had closed after himself when he took up position. He was to scram across the roof and down the furthest fire-escape – quick. I felt sorry for the kid, but Charlie said he was okay and mad keen to be blooded.

'I was to be inside the coffee-bar just before 10.30. If Slim, whom I was not to recognise in any way, lit the cigarette, I was to follow in a minute or two. Dodger was going to make his own way. He had been nicked in this neighbourhood before and was nervous. Once inside, he didn't mind.

'We were all to have a good meal. George's wife was providing sandwiches and flasks of tea. We had no idea how long we should take. It might be twelve hours, it might be through quickly. Again I wondered whether the kid on the roof would last out. I thought they were mad, but Jim said he was okay.

'The discotheque was blaring like crazy in the coffee bar when I arrived. I felt as sick as a cat. Slim, quite composed, was sitting in the window reading a newspaper and obviously studying form for the following week. He spent most of his time on this anyway. He glanced at his watch, smiled faintly and stubbed his cig. He looked at the paper again in a bored sort of way and then began to look down the street as if he was bird-watching. I gulped down my coffee, realised by the dregs that it had been in fact tea, and felt, rather than saw, the van go by. Slim's long legs uncurled. He beckoned the waitress, paid her with a bit of a flourish and went out. He paused – and lit a cigarette.

'I counted a hundred and twenty. Then I beckoned the girl. The street looked brighter than day. The flood of light in the closed Casbourne's window terrified me. Jim said that the window was cheap stuff. The real was well out of the reach of smash and grab – I went on.

'The little yard at the back was a pool of ink after the neon illumination of the street, but I could see the van, well back from the entrance, and turned for a quick getaway if anything should go wrong with the bells.

'The Law had been and gone. George was hunched over the wheel, only his eyes showing between scarf and hat. Shadows moved slightly and Jim's whisper placed him. Two more shadows. Charlie and his boy moved in. We put on our masks.

'The faint glimmer of a dimmed torch signalled that Slim was beginning the dicey work. On the door jamb, a small dot marked the bottom of the alarm button which could bring all hell about our ears. The top had been marked by him too. Now he was chipping a tiny sliver to admit a metal slide, fashioned from a screwdriver, just thick enough to hold the contact as the door opened. Dodger stood beside him, waiting for the signal for the key. I could feel the sweat under my shirt and, close to the van, smelt the sharp stink of George's fear.

'There was a tiny grunt from Slim, and Dodger bent over the lock. Suddenly there were steps round the corner. Jim opened the door of the van ready for flight – but it was only a couple. Slim was still holding the metal bar. The lock turned, and Dodger began with infinite care to open the door into the main building. There was not a sound.

'Dodger disappeared inside. Dodger reappeared with a grin and nodded to show he had drawn the fuse of that system. Now we lifted the rest of the gear through. We closed the door behind us and sent the kid up the inside staircase to keep his eyes skinned for the next few minutes when something might happen that we didn't know about. George would replace the sliver so that everything looked all right. We made for Casbourne's back door.

'We had got time now. Slim brought out a small drill and began work. He was confident that he could loop. This means that before you break the circuit of the alarm by cutting it, which would set it off, you loop one of the two wires above the point of entry to a bypassing one of higher resistance, joining it again below. You can then safely cut in, though you must repeat the drill every time you cross the system. We had been told that we should be able to draw the fuses in due course. It was a real education to watch Slim at work – it was just like a surgeon joining up. We were inside within minutes. It was barely eleven. We took off the masks.

'It's a funny thing, as Jim said, that the enemy always have a weak point. Casbourne's, once the outer defence was breached, hadn't got much of an inner guard. After all "They're often mean", said Charlie. There was a step halfway along the first vault which was ideal for the plank. From this, we could radiate off and we made a sort of island from which Jim and Dodger could go to work later on the main safe. Slim went ahead, checking each loop.

'This peter looked formidable and I wondered why Jim had been thumbs down on a thermic lance, except that they were rather sticky. But he knew, as usual. "They're just about to get a new one", he said. "Our boy at the makers told me. Let's look at its backside." He began to pick at the brickwork. Presently he said: "It's too thick here. Get into the next vault and cut in with Slim." It was nearly midnight. All the time, I kept hearing noises, but Jim was cool as cool and so were the others, though they were sweating a bit more than they should. I was in a fair bath but wouldn't admit it.

'Dodger and Charlie were sorting out loose silver, choosing the heaviest and least troublesome and stuffing it into sacks. We went behind, using a plank because there were some obvious tremblers there, and after a spot of picking, found the back of the safe a gimcrack job. "What did I tell you", said Jim. Slim said "See how the honest behave, doing the insurance! Fetch up the burners, Mike, and we'll have this little lot in a pig's whisper."

'Funny thing, Peta – I somehow expected Ali Baba's cave – all sparkles. Instead there were lots of little boxes, mostly old and rubbed – black and red and green. But this was the stuff. We began opening quickly, Jim and Dodger sorting as experts. There was some lovely stuff but every now and then they would grin and chuck a piece away, and these were the phoney ones that must have been flogged without the insurance knowing. "Wicked world", said Jim, grinning again like crazy. By now we were tiring and very thirsty but we wanted to be clear before full daylight. So I got the Thermoses out and found that one was bust to fragments and cut my hand deeply through the glove. But Jim said I could bloody well risk poisoning: no gloves off. We were near the end and Dodger slipped out with the piece of buff envelope for the door. We collected our gear and put it near the door. There were three sacks and a small briefcase. Jim said, looking round – "Only the best, mates."

'It was twenty to six when the slip went under the door. Six came and no George. Five past, ten past and we began to sweat. Then there was a scratching sound, Slim checked the bells and opened the inner door, and there he was, the van grey as a cat in the near dawn, its doors open right against the outer door. He had had the needle all right. As he came down the main street there had been two young Law bending down over the doorstep of the front entrance. By chance the slip had a figure 2 on it. It was probably thought to be a milk order. He hadn't known what to do but he cruised around for a few minutes and saw them move away and take no interest in the back of the premises. He waited till the coast was clear and then came round on foot. At the sight of the paper, he fled back to collect the van.

'We shoved it in like crazy, plus the bottles and gear, leaving nothing behind which could identify us. The kid came down from the roof, quite happy. Everything looked fine and we reckoned no one would be any the wiser till Monday. Slim and Dodger dropped off and made for home without a rock on them: they knew the value of being clean if they were turned over next week, and they had got first-class alibis. Jim and Charlie took the bags round to the drops. I took the few pieces which had been arranged and made for Heathrow. I'm not going to tell you how I got through because it's a bit too much of a trade secret.

'I can tell you those jewels burned a hole in my pocket. I was supposed not to make for Holland direct, just in case there was a follow-up; so I went by way of Stockholm, where my family had got friends, and had a few days there, with butter not melting in my mouth. I reckoned that to come back to England breaking the journey at Copenhagen and Amsterdam looked good enough even for Jim, so I did it this way, calling up a banking friend in Denmark and taking it easy.[8] The newspapers did us fairly well but things had quietened down by the time I contacted the Dutch fence, and I saw no sign of trouble at Schiphol – I reckoned they thought the stuff had either gone through or was stashed. He was sharp enough but scrupulously fair and I reckon he gave well over the tenth of the real value

[8] This incredible risk of running unnecessary Customs gauntlets shows that Michael was still something of an amateur.

we should have got in England. He was round and chubby, small for a Dutchman, and, the deal concluded, brought out the young Genever and talked shop. Quite interesting too – he had been taken for a ride in his youth by the "acky" trick – you know, switching the jar of nitric acid "aqua fortis" – hence the name for testing gold – for another and landing the dealer with duff ingots or rolled gold. He said it still works.

'Anyway, that's the Casbourne job. I enjoyed it. Dodger got nicked again and I hope he's got something to come out to – you never know. I only wish there was another coming along like it, because we were such good mates. But you feel pretty flat after it.'

Chapter 3

APPRENTICESHIP TO CRIME

How does the average young underworld recruit begin? 'Stole a bag of sweets when he was nine and never looked back', said one cheerful convict of another; and meant it. There was no sarcasm in the information. The small beginning is customary. In other worlds some may have greatness thrust upon them: in the underworld this is virtually unkown. Young Fred of Chapter 1 was born into an élite, that is to say a 'well-respected' underworld family; but his subsequent rating, like that of others, must be earned. The leader has to serve in the ranks before other crooks will trust him. Politicians urge honest men to progress by standing upon their own feet, and this admirable advice is faithfully followed by the villains, who are indeed one of the last bastions of unadulterated private enterprise left in the country, and who would go along with any exhortation about the undesirability of assisting lame ducks. The underworld, when it troubles to go to the poll, is solidly Tory, only wavering if there is any prospect of the Left turning up a Home Secretary more lenient to lawbreakers. And I am not being snide about it. In prison, a crook has no vote. Out of it, he belongs to the Right! However much he may work with a team from time to time, the crook is always a loner in the end, as the lame duck soon discovers. From the beginning, a boy learns, sometimes bitterly, that he is ultimately out on his own.

In John Gay's day and for a century after, many young thieves, as drawn in the character of Filch, were trained by women, and, shoplifting in the modern sense being unknown, in the absence of suitable shops, pickpocketing was a normal apprenticeship. Filch still exists as I realised recently. Emerging into the rain from a West End theatre where a reformed burglar and I had been revelling in an Alfred Marks farce, we were hailed by a shabby little man who knew J. The little man had a friend with a car round the corner who apparently would give us a lift. 'Decent of him' said J., pressing a generous tip into his hand. 'Taking up his time.' Our little acquaintance was 'working the crowds' – in short, pickpocketing, his speciality being theatre exit crushes – just as did Filch, outside the Opera House – and on a wet night! J., who although a reformed character is still well-respected, was pleased. The modern Filch had addressed him as 'Guv' and treated him right.

In John Gay's day, links between prostitution and thieving were extremely close. The brothels of Vinegar Yard (still existing in the City as a derelict alley) and Hockley-in-the Hole were filled with women who combined professional duties with stealing and especially with receiving. They were dubious allies to their male associates, often turning informer either to save their own necks or merely for profit. But co-operation continued. Most juvenile rogues did a spot of procuring on the side (also obliging the ladies of the town who could escape the rope if pregnant) and, one way and another, became familiar with all-round crime at an early stage on the inevitable progress to transportation or the gallows. Over the two centuries however, feminine participation in crime has shifted and, except for the family business, to be mentioned later, women and boys rarely work together nowadays.

The typical young delinquent who is not involved by family ties usually begins on shoplifting and store-breaking (which he does in association with other boys), looking as a rule for cigarettes, chocolate or other easily disposable loot; stealing objects of comparatively small value such as bicycles, and getting into mischief of a vandalistic type. Car offences of the 'driving and taking away without the consent of the owner' rather than permanent stealing are also common. The majority of boys who get into trouble (or even evade it at this stage) are not permanent underworld material, hooliganism and gang mischief being the dominant features; shoplifting is often a 'dare' – or competitive among rival gangs. But it is amongst these boys that a proportion of future crooks will be found; and there are quite a few men now in security prisons who were leaders of juvenile gangs.

Unfortunately, there is at present no reliable means of sorting out the merely mischievous boy from the dangerous material. The first hint of trouble and the lesson that crime does not pay, if it happens that way, winkles out many. Nature and events, sometimes sensible parents, thin out the ranks further, but some remain and go on to experiment with other aspects of crime. The worst thing that can happen to a boy is to get away successfully with his first crimes. It seems that the mediocre boy is the greatest risk, once started on delinquency. The highly intelligent boy rarely decides on crime as a future career. He does occasionally; but if he does so there are deep and real reasons for his decision. I can think of one tragic case of warped intelligence, much too well known to be identified here who would never have gone wrong in the absence of home stresses. The extremely stupid boy, on the other hand, is now better looked after by the community than he was. He may become a fall-guy or the unquestioning worshipper of an undesirable hero later on; but at the school age it is the boy with ambitions but no outstanding ability who tends to become a leader in mischief, since he may qualify as leader in this if nothing else. He is also, as recent research has shown, the most likely boy to get hooked on drugs, for precisely similar reasons.

Sooner or later, members of a gang get nicked. Some continue to get into mischief. After perhaps two or three attempts at probation, they pass inevitably into the care of the penal administration. This is where an apprenticeship to professional crime too frequently begins. It is not my purpose to criticise at this point the conduct of the Prison Department, however much tempted to do so; but that real life (and possibly preventable) contact with professional delinquency is found in every penal establishment is axiomatic: criminals who glory in their original sins will often tell with pride of the flying start given by chance meetings in the nick, Borstal, approved school or detention centre which happened to house them.[1] To give an example: South London today provides a field study for anyone who wishes to

[1] It is incidentally common practice for prison officers to make a special mark on the door of a cell which houses ex-Borstal boys who are usually regarded as potential trouble-makers.

trace the young rake's progress in the underworld. 'Drop a net over a circle two miles around Dulwich', said a graduate of Borstal, 'and you'd get the finest catch in England.' Not accurate; but the area *is* crammed with 30 – 40-year-olds who went to school together, got into mischief together, and then, via the various roads of imprisonment, met up with some of the worst company in the underworld and 'never looked back'. Some have got high up in their profession, and some have moved out of the district but return to familiar haunts for social links; most have formed the unskilled labour force of South London gangland. I never visit a prison without being primed with comradely messages from this part of London to friends inside: I never enter a spieler[2] south of the river without finding mutual acquaintances. One gave me a school group photograph. It might have been a football team: in fact, of the pleasant-faced boys therein depicted, every one has been in prison several times, some for grave and violent crimes, and one is an undoubted contestant for the title of worst gentleman of the London underworld today.

This is an extreme example but the pattern is depressingly familiar. Some of the boys who get into trouble come from criminal families and have a start by knowing mates 'inside' but others, deep in the misery of a first sentence, try to 'front' it out and it is they who, bragging about their minuscule hauls, are told by the more experienced prisoners of the big prizes that they can achieve. 'I remember', said one recidivist recently, 'how I was talking my big mouth off about the three hundred pounds my lot had cleaned up at the tobacconist's. "You don't want to think about peanuts like that", said Bob. "Why, when you come out, I'll fix for you to meet my 'minder'.[3] What do you think I'm in for? More than fifty grand; not your sort of lolly." And I can remember how fine he looked to me and how he did introduce me to his minder and I made a bomb.' (The bomb cost him, all told, some fourteen years on my reckoning but it would have done no good to refer to that.)

[2] 'Spieler' is London slang for betting-shop.

[3] 'Minder' – patron – often the gangster who sets up crimes for his protégés to carry out. Also used for the 'strong-arm' man who protects a patron.

'You want to graft proper' is what they hear. Too often, when they come out, they do join up with those who 'graft proper'. Prison is a sad and lonely place and the thought of a rich, adventurous and easy life afterwards is pleasant to contemplate in one's cell. Particularly in the miseries of a first sentence any friendly gesture seems a wonderful thing and the boy who is longing for sympathy is not well equipped to evaluate the company he keeps. I was told by some articulate young Dutch prisoners that the first three months of a first sentence are such a shock that a boy could probably be pulled up short, if properly handled at this stage. Then, progressively, he becomes used to prison and prison conditions: he ceases to mind so much and a subsequent sentence means little except as an interruption to life. I don't know how true this is: it seemed to make sense, even in a country which goes in for short sentences. What is axiomatic everywhere is that the hero, the most admired man in a prison is not, as a rule, its most admirable inhabitant in our sense of the term.

Whether a criminal career starts before or after contact with the law, progress thereafter is fairly stereotyped. One way or another, young A gets known as a sharper lad than young B. Probably at first he goes it alone or with another boy on small burglaries, stealing from lorries, hanging around dog-tracks or telephone booths for the odd handbag, carelessly left. But now it is not merely a mischievous gang activity. He is out to improve himself professionally. In spieler or pub, market-stall or the race-track, he is looking for a chance and, sooner or later, someone is going to notice him. He will be given a small job on a crime, perhaps only carrying a message, observing the time that someone leaves work or goes to a pub, the number of a lorry. If reliable, he may graduate to participation, for a slim young body can be inserted into a building with less trouble than a portly one and he will gradually learn the tricks of the trade: how to immobilise a simple alarm system, how to take a door off its hinges whilst keeping the alarms silent, how to muffle a 'jelly' job and the like. He will learn that women almost invariably keep valuables in the right-hand drawer of the dressing table; that before you nick a mink or sable coat you should slit the lining to make sure the furs are not tattooed with recognisable initials:[4] that porters take a kindly view of personable young men with a bunch of flowers (useful to conceal housebreaking implements also) and will frequently actually enlighten them as to who is in or out in a flat; that exquisite bathrooms in expensive premises often contain the safe concealed behind tiles; and that ex-employees of security device makers are pure underworld gold if, that is, they are corruptible. A myriad such scraps of underworld knowledge will be coming his way whilst he begins to develop some speciality, of which the most prized today is to drive the escape car. And all the time he will be observed and spoken of. He will not be above minor protection rackets and may be used by the bigger boys to 'collect rents', i.e. protection money, a form of underworld *Danegeld,* which has existed since time immemorial and only attracts public notice when it becomes too greedy. He will probably run a tiny racket himself. He will be extremely lucky if he escapes the notice of the law.

As his skill and confidence grow and if his reputation is good, he will begin to pick up colleagues. Fifty years ago, these might well have been lifelong associations: today's more complicated and specialised crime-scene does not lend itself to a criminal David and Jonathan act. But men of the underworld, as in the outer world, tend to ally themselves with similars and X, Y and Z whose methods accord with each other are likely to find themselves recruited on to the same jobs on numerous occasions. So an existing gang renews itself and is self-perpetuating.

It is, I think, when the recognition of 'We' and 'They', mentioned before, establishes itself that the young crook really passes into permanent crime: permanent, that is, unless something happens to change his ways. Otherwise, from now on, he will persistently work to improve his techniques and will probably model himself on his most admired villain, for all notable leaders have their fans. The intelligent young crook has to choose between the big stuff – banks, jewellery, bullion (airport- or van-snatched

[4] One old hand tells a sad story of how, in his youth, he stole two sable coats from a well-known actress. When he took the 'pussies' (the underworld nickname for furs of any kind) to the fence, he was contemptuously rebuffed. Every skin was tattooed with her initials and the coats ended up on the fire, for nobody would touch them.

mainly today) and the pursuit of small, everyday burglaries, quick snatches from hotels and the like; though even top thieves can seldom resist a tempting little bargain since opportunism plays a continual part in dishonest careers. A very 'top-boy' was driving slowly down Park Lane not so long ago with a friend, bound for a cosy chat in the bar of Grosvenor House, when he saw a magnificent mink coat over the shoulders of a girl who had not got her arms into the sleeves. It was irresistible. Asking the friend to slow down and be ready to make a dash for it, he slipped from the car, snatched the coat and was away before the girl realised it had gone. This episode was admired and was also reckoned very funny, though he was thought to have lost a certain amount of 'class' in coming down to a lower type of thieving. 'Funny, but out of his class' was the general verdict.

'Good'-class burglaries, however, can indeed be profitable and an astonishing number of these go unreported. Numbers of people keep large sums of cash in the house, unreported, to the tax authorities. The up-and-coming thief today has to do his homework on this score and others.

A young criminal born into a criminal family, as we have seen, slides into crime without noticing it, since it is instilled into him with his mother's milk. Just as the young of certain animals know instinctively that they must lie silent and still when predators are around, so children of crooked families grow up with the underworld lore as everyday pabulum. At an early age they can be valuable assets to the family. As already said, a small child can be pushed through a skylight or small ventilation window where an adult cannot pass;[5] but a youngster can also carry a message or a packet without arousing suspicion: I have known a child used as a lookout. Until recently – the custom decreased for a time – a common way of breaking in a child to a future of professional crime was the travelling shoplift. I am told that there are signs of a revival.

This highly-developed and skilled exercise involved whole families. The father often opted out, possibly because other professional duties intruded, or because his face was well known.

[5] The cautious householder should always consider the dimensions of these and put a cross-bar when necessary.

Mother, children, often aunts and uncles and a few friends on occasion used to set off by car to tour the country, pillaging shops on the way. Routes were regular and the operation well-planned. Starting from London, Birmingham might be the first port of call, then Manchester, the department stores of the district, perhaps Liverpool and then home. Next week, the East or the West of the country would be visited, with the possibility of a day or two by the sea thrown in. The storage places of loot varied: sometimes it was with accomplices in the district visited and the young learned to help by watching and then by active participation, diversionary tactics being the essence of a successful heist. Also, as they learned the means of disposal (predominantly through dishonest stallholders in markets, but also with specialised fences), they were picking up future acquaintances of value for bigger gains later on. The provinces did the route in reverse to include London, and 'manors' were carefully allotted and respected. I have always thought that this activity may have had its routes in gypsy origins, and it is a fact that gypsy surnames are common among thieves.

This, the most recent example of women training young thieves, temporarily less common possibly because of Australian competition, has kept shoplifting in higher regard in the underworld than it might otherwise be. 'Taught by me Mum' is still proudly reported and there are some redoubtable Mums in underworld history. My husband on occasion used to defend one Maggie Hughes, queen of her craft in her day, a passionate animal-lover who was prone to fly out from her house to belabour any coster she considered to be overloading his donkey on 'her' hill. Maggie, no sylph, was the terror of Oxford Street shops, owing to her skill in concealing two fur-coats at a time (her speciality) beneath her skirt, on a stout elastic band; and then strolling unconcernedly to the exit. She was fond of my husband, who had extricated her from several awkward situations with minimal penalty, and even fonder of a famous Counsel of his day, the late G. L. Hardy, who had appeared for her and a number of her active relatives. 'Give you a good piece of advice, dears', she said to them gratefully one day. 'Same as I always tell the nippers. Never leave an empty 'anger.' To this day, if I leave a fitting-room wherein there is an empty 'anger, it passes through my mind that I might be suspected!

Anyway, it seems that where shoplifting is concerned – which is in England the form of theft favoured by women, though by no means exclusive to them – it is where the children of the underworld parents often get their first practice runs. Eventually, however, all meet up 'on the job' and whether inherited or acquired, the developed skills of dishonesty progress from the general to the specialised practice.

It would be wrong to leave this subject with the suggestion that an overwhelming majority of the children of criminals drift into crime. In most respectable families there is a black sheep somewhere. In the underworld it is the 'white' sheep who brings the shame and distress – the distorted mirror-image of the other world indeed. Eventually a well-to-do member of the family who has left the nest for a respectable life may come to be thought well of: a husband or wife may also rue the day when he or she married into a family whose members require bailing out at awkward moments or the respectable one may decide, as many have done, to emigrate and cut off from the old ties. Usually, however, it is the family which does the separating. Sometimes a story is told one which is so corny that it is difficult to believe it really happened but the fact is that a lot of underworld life is very corny indeed. 'You'd never believe what that girl of mine has done', said a sorrowing acquaintance to me some months ago, raising his head from the large Scotch he had ordered as prophylactic against his state of shock (though not too shocked to charge it to me!) 'Came back last night and' – here he looked round to see that the four walls concealed no listening ear – 'broke her mother's heart she did.' Mother had been to my certain knowledge a rare old grafter and occasional ponce until her retirement as an alcoholic, and it was difficult to imagine just what *could* damage that sturdy organ. Had the daughter been nicked? 'Nicked!' groaned Papa, 'I only wish she had. No. I'll give you a fiver if you can guess. The little cow', he went on quickly in case I might win the fiver, 'she's got herself mixed up with the Law. Says she's going to marry a copper! I never thought her mother and I would live to see the day. *Marry*! I ask you!

Why can't she just work it out of her system? It's a free country isn't it? Oh no – it's got to be a white wedding and all, if you please. Marry indeed! I shall never have a moment's peace. Talk about bringing trouble on a decent family!' He looked at me suddenly with a brighter expression. 'Maybe that Law of hers can be straightened. What do you think?' Optimists, these villains.

Chapter 4

VILLAINS À LA MODE

To understand the influences which have worked on young Fred and his contemporaries, we have to put a magnifying glass over recent underworld history. The hard core of any underworld consists of the thieves. When crime is the chosen means of making a living, stealing is the most obvious way it is done, producing in its turn a number of ancillary crimes which develop because of it. We live in an increasingly complicated world and the social upheaval which has gone on over the past quarter of a century has affected this hard core of the underworld as profoundly as it has done the other strata of society. Education, the levelling out of social classes, increased affluence, the enlarged horizons that go with it have all played their part. So has a general alteration in public and private morality. Whilst 'the criminal' is still the whipping-boy of society, he has become, in his new guise, much more *socially* acceptable, because he looks it.

The race-course, for example, continues to be a favoured haunt of criminals, but nowadays some at least will aspire to the most expensive enclosures, and few will fall below a high standard of sartorial elegance.[1] (I have come to regard a superfluity of hand-stitching on a suit as marking either crook or CID off-duty nowadays.) Gambling is an almost whole-time leisure pursuit in the underworld, where huge sums of money change hands all the time and burglaries can be committed merely to pay for this luxury. Gambling takes thieves into the clubs and casinos : money – and the wages of successful dishonesty are high – into the best hotels and into restaurants which, a quarter of a century ago, would not have admitted old Fred, who would have been scared

[1] No longer charging round racecourses with hatchets as, in his day, did a mild old fellow who is the uncle of one of the most formidably violent criminals today!

anyway.[2] I have kept assignations with the underworld in most of the 'grand' spots of London. I have also been turned out with one of them; but only because he was wearing a polo-neck in the bar, a very expensive pure silk one, underneath a well-cut hacking-type jacket. He was one-up in the end however. He turned on his way out and said with dignity to the waiter, 'I don't mind being inconvenienced myself so long as *you* keep up your standards!' And to me he said very audibly, 'I must apologise for this sort of thing. We'll go and drink our champagne elsewhere.' Which we did.

When we congratulate ourselves smugly upon the improved social conditions of our time, think how nice it is that class barriers are down and take for granted that the Archers drink champagne at parties instead of the beer (possibly herb) of a century ago, it is easy to forget that there are two sides to every aspect of progress. Gone are the old-school-tie barriers: the most peculiar people, in clothes that would once have seemed rank indecency, throng royal enclosures and royal occasions. Dukes have gone into show business and Cockney millionaires abound. In all this there is one 'Open Sesame'. Modern society, for all practical purposes, is based on money; and the underworld has not been long in catching on to the idea. It is a very good idea from their point of view. What it means in practical terms is that, for the first time in British history at least, a crook is as good as his money; and provided his wallet is well stuffed, he will be welcome in the top spots of the world, where hoteliers and *restaurateurs* will skip to his call. In the last few years a new snobbism has arisen. It has become a prestige symbol in 'smart' circles to be in cahoots with gangsters. Considering how gormless is much of their 'communication', as we now call it, this is puzzling to anyone who, like myself, has had contact for a long time. But there it is. It is a fact of life.

The roots of this may lie in the comparative safety of modern life. The underworld ticks on greed, as it has always done, every-

[2] A dear old veteran, 'inactive' for many years, was brought to a café by a nephew, to tell me some tales of the old days. The nephew ordered three Welsh rabbits. A look of great disappointment spread over the old man's face. 'I don't see any rabbit in mine', he said.

where. But there is a percentage of underworld characters who begin a half-hearted criminal career with a warped sense of adventure. Whatever you may feel morally about burglary, it *is* more interesting than, say, punching out a hole in metal eight hours a day. In the film industry for instance (where fringe characters abound as extras and hanging-about occupies far more time than work), educated but bored people starting talking to these strangers and are brought into contact with what sounds like exciting adventure. Race-courses, whether horse, motor or dog, are other points of meeting: so are the pubs and clubs. A comparatively innocent yearning for kicks can take youngsters into smuggling; but what begins as a lark, such as running dirty books to France ('You want the finest dirt: we have it!') can end as blackmail and worse. This sort of temptation is understandable. In a world where we never had it so good or so spoon-fed, the 'excitement' of crime may well seem alluring: from our nursery days, Robin Hood, Ned Kelly and Dick Turpin have been acclaimed. The draw of walking through Mayfair, arm-in-arm with self-styled protection kings, remains inexplicable. Unhappily, it is true.

The social class of people who commit crimes is now definitely higher in the scale than it used to be. The sons of the racecourse gangs have had, via education, the opportunity to become white-coated technicians: some may have brought shame upon a good family by going straight but others have seen the possibilities of knowing how to operate thermic lances and similar toys; and there is, by repute, one such who works a full day in perfectly upright business but takes a whacking consultancy fee in safety as an adviser on ways and means of entering strong rooms. 'I wanted to know what the best methods of dealing with modern safes were', (well, this was not quite what another said, but his remark was a bit unprintable), 'so I sent the son to night-school.' 'Joe's wife's young brother got something called "A" levels. He's going to work in a bank for a bit. Reckons it will come in useful.' In these circles this view is fair enough. What worries the sociologist is the number of 'respectable' people who allow themselves to be corrupted in ways other than fraud, a white-collar offence mainly, which for some reason or other has always been considered less culpable than common theft, especially by those who commit it. One of my husband's clients, charged with stealing, maintained that he was of good character. Under cross-examination, he admitted to a conviction for false pretences. 'That's not dishonesty', he said indignantly. 'Dishonesty is when you pinches it, and in this case the mug gives it to you.'

If money talks to the underworld, it talks to a lot of other people too. Old Fred, as related, used to watch 'his' premises. Modern criminals rarely need to do so. Someone will give them the information they want; and a number of people will now do the job for reward. A gold-van is to be robbed; it is some clerk employed somewhere along the route, who will sell just the one scrap of vital information about timing or calls that enables a successful snatch. A jeweller's is to be entered. Someone is prepared to sell his integrity and to remove a fuse from the alarm system for those vital ten minutes when the entry is made. There are few raids of any size where most of the necessary information has not been obtained by buying it (though sometimes moronic people have unwittingly shot off their big mouths in the wrong place – newspaper offices are often guilty of this), and even fewer really big hauls made without the assistance of the gang's 'bell-man', the man who silences the alarms. He has often been a man of good character, employed by a firm who makes or minds alarms; and he is well fitted to sell his employers down the river. He will crop up again as well as the whole subject of corruption and if I appear to repeat myself on this, it is because corruption today creeps in so repeatedly.

It is when the 'big boys' want to move into something really huge that corruption happens on an unusual scale. The reason for this is mainly economic. Major crime being more sensationally profitable than it used to be, the prosperous thief can bribe more effectively. When big loot is to be shifted 'someone in the City' with acess to Swiss bank accounts (many Big Boys have got their own but an alibi is always useful), crooked lawyers and dubious international 'journalists', are contacted and used. The enormous extension of the *Corps Diplomatique* has brought into the service of some foreign embassies commercial attachés, *n*th grade, whose professional standards are quite different from those of their predecessors. (One has only to look at what has been found in diplomatic luggage in the States to verify this.) These are all people who belong to professions whose ethical codes they simply ignore and it is often very difficult for the police to 'break' their identities. The odd black sheep has always existed in all walks of life. What a changing underworld knows full well is that old barriers are now down. Recruits to crime are now much more easily come by. Just now and again, someone will do it for kicks and kicks alone; ninety-nine per cent and more do it for a shareout. These are the people who have given the underworld its latest ideas. The dreary old long-firm fraud used to be about the limit of their financial ambitions:[8] in the past year or two, we have seen the spectacle of criminals moving in on the world of international frauds and getting away with it.

This is not to say that (minus cloth caps) the less affluent layers of the underworld do not exist. They do indeed: they complain bitterly of being skint at intervals: it is a long time since I have seen any family there in real want and no one is round to Social Security more quickly for basic necessities, whilst an erring father is borrowing money for his defence or, hopefully, for bribing the police. It is a true measure of change in the underworld. Like his respectable counterpart, and his successful colleague, the relatively humble criminal has leapt the class barrier. He considers himself as good as anyone else, and he expects society to support him, as legal aid most certainly does. The better equipped thief has upped his social image in other ways. He wants to *look* respectable, mainly for professional reasons but with some odd quirks to his ambition. One of the robbers of Mail Train fame is said by his friends to have been the inventor of the businessman cover for the professional criminal; setting out in the morning as a respectable City type, bowler, black jacket and pinstripes, briefcase and the lot; so that the neighbours have no idea of the Jekyll-and-Hyde nature of quiet young men. One such partnership might have been the original screen-play of *The*

[8] The long-firm fraud is a popular and easy way of making money – till found out. It consists of setting up premises and acquiring goods on credit, selling them quickly and disappearing. The process is often repeated in other districts.

Ladykillers. Their early exploits often involved posing as young music students, complete with violin-cases – a handy shape for carrying rather bulky packages; and coming home late at night thus equipped suggesting a return from concert or restaurant, rather than robbery. Certainly something about the new generation has helped to confuse the image and, in a curious way, to mark a change in underworld attitudes, some crooks behaving as if the assumed cloak is wanted as a way of separating home and 'business'. 'He never brings his *work* home', said an angry wife, angry because she had been turned over, i.e. had her house searched, early that morning and it is difficult to account to the neighbours for a couple of Squad cars at your door at 7 a.m. 'Whatever shall I do if the *Surrey Comet* gets hold of it', wailed another wife, horrified by the social consequences of a husband about to appear in the dock at the Old Bailey. 'Next door's a bank manager who's often talking about burglars and I've always told them Tom was something in the City. He and his wife are in and out of our swimming-pool all the time and I don't know what he'll say.' Problems of the affluent underworld indeed! The *Surrey Comet*, as it happened, missed that one; but there are many 'businessmen' in the immediate suburbs of London and other cities who set out daily on a very different work schedule from that in which the neighbourhood has been led to believe.

Travel has been one of the most profound influences. The prosperous thief with ambitions has been whooping it up for years on the sunny beaches of the Cote d'Azur, Costa Brava and Majorca, and visiting successful gangsters with villas in Tangier. No travel restrictions existed for these explorers who were, in any case, often on holidays with pay, picking up gold and silver from incautious visitors. Indeed, the 'Continental holiday', which soon became a joke in the underworld, spread so rapidly, sideways and downwards, that professional rules had to be created, since poaching on others' manors started up rows and, on one occasion, led to a killing. It was certainly an attractive idea to lie upon warm beaches, do a little gambling ('Give me the Sporting Club for preference but there's *class* at Monte!' said one) and pay for the whole outing, with a little something in the pocket, all for one night's work. The hotels got wise to a few incautious ones

('I am *persona non "gratin"* at the Carlton in Cannes', another remarked to me, rather engagingly); but the skilful ones survived and began to make working arrangements with the locals.

The results of this have not been funny. Links had existed for a long time in the highest échelons of crime, (that is to say, the jewel thieves), by which London and Paris assisted each other and, more particularly, 'fenced' to mutual advantage the results of theft and fraud in Hatton Garden (the centre of the London jewel trade) and Paris. A favourite trick is for a Continental operator to come over to Hatton Garden and, rather late in the day, after the banks are shut, to ask to see diamonds of an exact weight and quality. He selects a number, has them made up into a packet and asks that they should be kept for him to pick up and pay for the next day. Diamonds are always packed in a certain blue-tinted paper and, at this point, the thief, who knows the exact weight and size and has prepared in advance an identical package filled with carefully weighed rubbish, distracts the seller's attention and switches the two. The bogus one goes into the seller's safe and the next morning the buyer fails to turn up. By the time the false packet is opened, the thief, who has caught the previous evening's plane[4] to Paris or elsewhere, is untraceable. But quite often the diamonds are fenced over here, as the thief may not wish to pass the Customs, and in return may extend the same courtesies to his obliging English friends.

Some of these 'partnerships' almost achieved respectability (they certainly did in the underworld!) by virtue of long-standing loyalty and a high degree of technical skill. It is well known that the majority of jewel transactions in the trade were made and remained binding by word of mouth : the keeping of documentary evidence necessitated by gold and currency restrictions always cut across this freemasonry of the trade. It had its counterpart in the underworld where, say a quarter of a century ago, some of the closest genuine friendships were to be found among the thieves who operated between London, Paris and Amsterdam. I am often shown, for example, tattered photographs produced

[4] The train used to be popular. But they say that high-class thieves don't like the noise of the Cross-Channel Ferry.

from wallets of a Pole, resident in Paris, who was until his death a few years ago, so genuinely beloved among his associates that he is, quite literally, never forgotten – something rare in the ever-dissolving picture of the underworld. This sort of attachment was not, of course, universal – far from it. But the fact that it needed skill, courage and co-operation all tended to draw in a better (if that be the word) class of criminal than the average. Anyway, the reader can see the point.

Now everything erupted. Travel conditions were revolutionised. British and Continental thieves were suddenly cheek by jowl and the world of crime that opened before British eyes was something that few of them had seen before.

The underworld of the Mediterranean littoral makes the London gangs[5] appear, by contrast, innocents abroad. The coverage given by the Press to the Richardson and Kray cases is evidence that, although we have our moments crime-wise, the public (even those who enjoy a degree of sadism in their reading) can still be shocked by the relation of what these cases involved. What happens several times a week in the hills behind the smiling coastline from Villefranche to Marseilles would keep an English crime-reporter busy for a month. Murder has always been traditionally disliked in the English underworld, not so much on moral grounds (capital punishment is by no means disapproved of there) but because a murder-hunt tends to be used by the police as a happy chance for 'turning over' suspects connected with other crimes. Murder, in short, is a nuisance and makes trouble for everyone. Still, there is a certain taboo attached to killers, not always as strong as that which attached to one Eddie who escaped from Devil's Island and was always referred to as 'Him that ate his Mates'. It is a somewhat wobbly taboo and 'He had to go' is a common euphemism for the removal of unpopular figures, said without much horror. Or another macabre phrase, used from the eighteenth century onwards: 'His time had come', makes one's blood run cold at the casual tone of the remark. But

[5] Throughout the book, unless otherwise defined, the word 'gang' is used in its English sense, i.e. a number of men working together at any one time. 'Gangster', American, has a totally different meaning and is frequently and unjustly used of English criminals to imply violence. There are few 'gangsters' in this country, though they are on the increase.

killing, except in the way of vital business, such as the cosh which falls too hard on the the head of a nightwatchman, which is generally thought to be unprofessional and a pity (but not really culpable) is not popular. Informants, even those who do not play it both ways and are therefore useful, live to sneak another day. It is impossible to envisage a Corsican allowing such wrongs to go unavenged.

Murder is accepted on the Mediterranean littoral as a matter of course. So is every kind of violence, sex-crime and drug-offence. The first impact of this on the visiting British thief was one of shock. I have never seen anyone more outraged than a lorry hi-jacker who discovered that rape was quite a usual method of ensuring in Sicily that the girl of your choice would have to marry you. The same disapproval used to apply to drug carrying, which went on in a small way but was relegated to the lowest ranks of the fraternity – and the caste system of the underworld could give points to most others. Familiarity however breeds not only contempt but indifferences. The observation of big money made by crimes which had previously been frowned upon in England was having its effect. Toleration of much more sinister crime was being established.

All this was, of course, a slow and gradual process and is still going on. What crystallised it was the coincidence that a series of very successful robberies here, hotly pursued by Scotland Yard, made it convenient for the thieves to link with the Continental underworld, who were experienced not only in fencing but in arranging quick getaways for men on the run. The ports of the Mediterranean hold many small gangs who specialise in smuggling loads across to Africa, whether men or materials; and the fact that British villains were ready to pay and pay well set the ball rolling. Not that these gangs are always reliable. They cheat, betray and, on occasion, have been known to drown customers. But interests are usually sufficiently mutual to ensure reasonably straight dealing.

There is never a clear-cut picture of anything in any underworld. As in a muddy aquarium you see, from time to time, a fish flash by, perhaps pursued by another but always moving, changing, but in the mud and swirling water. So it is with the Mediterranean underworld, perhaps even more than with most others. It is territory through which or near to which the main drug traffic passes, either as morphine-base (on its way to the Middle East to the clandestine laboratories outside Paris or in the hills behind the coastline), or returning as heroin, to be smuggled to the United States, Canada or other destinations by all means of transport. Where drugs can be smuggled, men can be passed along, as if on a giant relay-race for a high fee, on which there is a cut, the contact's 'masters' taking the rest. There is nothing new in this except British participation and a lot of it goes on. A man who has worked reliably for the Mafia over a number of years gets retained by them, but is allowed to freelance, as it were, when he is not wanted for anything else, within reason and so long as interests do not clash. The unskilled criminal labour pool of this region consists mainly of Corsicans, Algerians and expatriate Italians: there are some French, though this, French colonial policy being what it is, covers some racial and colour admixture. The French tend to get the better jobs and supply the links to higher up the scale, and they probably also supply most of the planning in this area. Mafia and its hirelings in this region make rings round the local police: it is usually Interpol who bring off the 'kills', to be publicised a day or two later in *Nice-Matin* as 'Great Drug Haul': nice reading for the tourist whilst Mafia shrugs off the loss of money and manpower (knowing that there is plenty more where both came from), but holds careful inquests, in case any leakage has to be dealt with, in which event somebody has an 'accident'. There is no trespassing with impunity on Mafia manors: one leading British gangster found this to his cost when, having sent a deputy to clean up on a theft, and having been welshed by the deputy, he flew out to take vengeance and was himself fined for the whole amount, under threat of severe mutilation. The echoes of this are still ringing loudly, both fleecer and fleeced being in prison on long sentences for different offences, but still threatening each other by the agency of friends, who, like most of the underworld, enjoy keeping things going. In passing, it may be noted that there is no finer bush-telegraph than in the South of France. Every criminal happening within Europe and a lot more from elsewhere is known within a short space of time, and I can testify that information from these rather scruffy sources is remarkably accurate.

Contact with the shady Mediterranean, and eventually the American world, was increased by the fantastic growth of gambling in Britain which followed the Gaming act. Britain has on the whole escaped the attentions of Mafia so far by virtue of one simple fact: we are not a large enough market to attract them. Like the Germans of whom Tacitus remarked *'Ubi praeda, ibi patria'* ('Where there is booty, there is their fatherland'), Mafia will only move in where the pickings are big enough, be it gambling or undertaking, (for death is one sure bet as a business); and for a couple of years it looked as though the betting which had mushroomed around British casinos was worth American Mafia's while. The police did their best but it is difficult to keep tabs on every Boeing-load of tourists ostensibly bound for a few days' gambling in London casinos; and many a well-known American member of Cosa Nostra found it easy to slip past immigration for a few days, setting up or visiting on arrival stooge directors so that a move-in was easy at any time. One of the best-known characters in the London underworld has a retainer to watch Mafia interests and to lay out small salaries for bogus directors. The wages of this corruption are not very high: surprisingly £200 – 300 per annum seems about average, tax-free naturally. Danger of gambling club takeovers seems to be past, though the set-up still exists and could be quite easily used for large drug operations or anything else that turned up. It is tempting to think that this is already happening with drugs; but the necessary involvement of the professional underworld does not really exist at the moment, though it is anyone's guess as to the future. The residual harm, once more, is familiarity, together with the knowledge that big money, that irresistible fools' gold of the underworld, is tied up with American contacts. A few of the fraternity already carry drugs on occasion. As they are often twisted over transactions, enthusiasm tends to wane, but this tendency is liable to escalate at any time.

All told, international contacts have not done our villains any good. The Commonwealth never has. Much of the profitable know-how in crime this century has been worked out by the

Australians; as always, professionals in everything they do. Even the celluloid strip to open Yale locks originated 'down under'. They perfected the 'con-trick' and during the past few years Australian shoplifters have appeared on the scene to win the ungrudging admiration of their British counterparts:[6] they have gone on to master-mind a number of other crimes. The arrival of the Australian contingents coincided with a moment when the London underworld was suffering its worst withdrawal symptoms from the absence of a top gang in the capital: 'Pommy' villains were soon given a transfusion of vitality and renewed ambition. One effect has been to teach our underworld a new technique practised by the shoplifters which makes police investigation still more difficult. Drawing on large numbers of personnel (but always in different small groups) to commit any large-scale crime, they avoid recognition of well-known faces – a factor which has been the undoing of many small gangs over here. Re-grouping is now being used a great deal. By the time the Australians had turned their attention to other crimes (at the time of writing they have a large measure of control in the art and antique robberies and are up to something unspecified on the Continent which involves the recruitment of the few remaining French cat-burglars), they had also set a further example of violence to the younger underworld whose results we are seeing today. (The underworld attitude to violence altogether is something which must be considered on its own, though it keeps on cropping up.) The Australians are not exactly gentle. They have a contact over here who works so hard on their behalf (not without reward) that he is practically their Public Relations Officer.[7] Slightly nervous of some information I possessed, this gentleman said to me 'For God's sake don't mention Australians on this job or I'm history!'

No one knows just why violence has mushroomed in the past decade. It is a world-wide phenomenon. One or two local factors, however, have affected Britain. Ironically, increased police

[6] I was told by the host that at a dinner-party, given by classy underworld for visiting Aussie shoplifters, the visitors bet that they could get away with something under four pairs of experienced eyes. They did. Ten minutes after departure, they returned with a clock – and it wasn't a small one.

[7] When I mentioned this fact to a guileless colleague, he said 'Goodness! Do they employ a PRO?'.

efficiency is one. The hated 'Panda', replacing the man on the beat whose routine could be known and planned for: two-way radios, which enable a hidden watcher to summon Squad cars without any overt warning: improved alarm systems which function covertly – everything in short which has made the old, slow, well-cased weekend robbery on the site a more difficult proposition, has led to the conclusion that the only weak spot to attack valuables is in transit: to attack in transit always means violence and someone is sure to get hurt even when the almost inevitable corruption eases things up. 'I always listen to the Metropolitan and Surrey lot' explained one thief, who has recently adopted more violent methods than in the past. 'You should hear the special loads stuff, particularly the GPO and the airport convoys, but the tip-off is usually okay.'

One cannot be entirely happy either about the effect of punitive sentences. Many judges maintain that by long sentences they are showing that crime does not pay. It may have this effect on the particular prisoner in the one instance but if there is one thing for sure in the underworld, it is that they do not, in that school, learn by the experience of others. 'They' will always be cleverer. What long sentences have done in many cases is to ensure that men, particularly the rising generation, going on a job, carry guns. 'When you got a five', has been said many times, 'what was the use of coshing a guard and getting extra bird?' 'But now', added one thief who has yet no violence in his substantial record, 'if I reckoned I was going to get the sort of bird that's going to be dished out to me, I'd carry a gun and use it.' Fortunately for the community this particular one has struck lucky on car sales and plans to retire but there are many who have not. 'I don't want to kill nobody', said another, 'but it don't make sense to get the sort of stretch they gave Jack.' This sounds like an argument for capital punishment. If you come to think it out, it is exactly the opposite. These are the *older* ones speaking: the ones who used to regard a gunman with horror. Today few young criminals go out unarmed, and middle-aged ones are beginning to follow suit. Some youngsters do it from fashion and bravado. Unhappily, many a boy has fired in fright a gun which he did not really intend to use. Most have no such compunction, anyway. Amphetamine, the drug first used by the escape-driver who is the hero of many young crooks, has increased violent tendencies, its properties being more deadly than alcohol since they actually affect personality, not merely enhance it; and its widespread use shocks and terrifies that older portion of the underworld who know even better than we do the acceptance of violence as a fact of underworld life. But oldsters are dying out or in retirement. Violence is part of today everywhere, and the underworld is no exception to the rule. It was never a place to romanticise but things today have certainly reverted nearer to the barbarity of the eighteenth and nineteenth centuries.

Any account of the changing face of the London underworld would be incomplete without some comment on the effects of the successful smashing of that top gang whose activities culminated in the Mail Train robbery: the laws of libel forbid any linking of other exploits with those who worked with it from time to time; but it can be assumed that the active members were so well known to the police that they were understandably anxious to get as many as possible of them behind bars for a long time –an ambition partially fulfilled at least. The results were not quite as beneficial as law and order had hoped. To understand the effect on the underworld, one has to accept their viewpoint, not ours, and to realise that whilst the gaoling of major and skilful criminals may seem a triumph for the forces of respectability –and sometimes is – the effect on other criminals may be quite different.

The underworld needs a king to hold it in check. In our case it also seems to need a top gang, to work with whom brings prestige (and, naturally, profit) while from the police point of view it is actually convenient to know whom to 'turn over' instantly when a large crime has been committed and to be able to keep tabs on new associates. Hence the reason for the new Australian tactics referred to earlier in the chapter. Most people in underworld circles had a good idea as soon as the Mail Train job was done as to who was likely to have been involved, even though the secret had been closely guarded. From the robbers' point of view, considering the care taken prior to the crime, it was singularly bad luck that their precautions against identification went astray; but I remember clearly that although the job had been kept as close as Operation Cicero, 'Couldn't be anyone else but . . .' was being said in every spieler within hours. At the time I wrote somewhere or other – it was merely repetition of what informed sources had said to me – that the result of smashing this particular gang would lead to a situation in the underworld when the scum would rise to the top – and they did. A top gang, with all its attendant tiresomeness, big robberies and the like, helps to keep the underworld in check. It is prestigious to work with them: professional pride tends to make a team good technicians instead of merely thugs: everyone is interested in getting in on the act, even to the extent of going to night-school to perfect knowledge to be used to ends not envisaged by the authorities. A top-gang, so far as any order can be maintained in this anarchical society, at least ensures discipline in patches and rather less violence over-all. There is a moral somewhere in the keep-fit, cold bath, running in the park in the morning, gymnasium work-outs, etc. imposed upon the lieutenants of the really top crooks, even if it is just professionalism. The last few years have seen a state of anarchy in the underworld which has been no good to anyone. Internecine scrapping, young crooks with nothing but the immediate grab in front of them and with no need to impress eyes watchful for apprentices (who would have to learn obedience to the rules of 'good' work): an immediate rise in protection rackets, from the more publicised ones down to the petty £10-a-week-and-drinks-and-eats-on-the-house put over by innumerable little crooks who went round frightening landlords with tales of mythical violence to be – all these were soon to be seen. No-account boys became fruit-machine tycoons – and hired thugs to beat up trespassers. It was the underworld rather than the respectable who marvelled (whilst enjoying the pickings!) at the incredible folly of the Gaming Act and its timing: 'Must be in the pay of someone', was the usual comment on our legislators. London has not yet recovered and there is still no king.

However, amongst many aspirants a new gang is emerging, not so violent in its beginnings as might have been feared, though pretty tough. It consists of some half-dozen under-thirties, all from the East End, all skilful and all with social ambitions as well as professional ones. The police apparently know their identities but have so far been unable to make arrests. The only name I have heard for them is 'The Likely Lads' and they have reputedly been making a bomb. Gang meetings are kept well away from home territory and already many younger criminals are reported to be keen to be taken on as hands. The grapevine says that guns have appeared recently. This gang may be nipped in the bud: it may go on to establish some sort of domination over the criminal scene. So far as I can discover at the moment, it is run on reasonably democratic lines with majority votes on general principles (as was the South-Western gang responsible for the Great Mail robbery, though this definitely had a chief): no overall leader has emerged in the new one as yet. It would be a good thing on the whole if this gang could keep down some of its worst rivals, except for the inescapable fact that 'we' are going to lose a lot of money to anything so successful. But even as one writes, there are reports of three more challenging groups, one of which is said to have 'done' a robbery in Lloyds' Bank in Baker Street, using a walkie-talkie radio which was picked up in nearby Harley Street. My telephone must have grown warm with the comments which flowed in following this. First of all, there was praise from professionals for the cheek and skill. However, when it became clear that they had acually used each other's *names*, condemnation was universal and comical. 'Innocent as new-born babes', said one. 'Don't they know nothing? Why we was taught before we was let out on a job that it was numbers and nothing else and we didn't have BBC equipment.' 'I remember', said another 'getting a clip on the earhole for saying a name, the first job I ever did.' So it went on. I recollected that an old shoplifter had complained, a few days previously, that the thieves today were averse to apprenticeship. She was obviously right.[8]

These reflections are not sarcastic. Comedy does creep in on the underworld as elsewhere in real life. But we must face the fact that armed robbery is now the norm of young offenders. One is therefore sometimes faced with a Hobson's choice and I person-

[8] These, as it proved, were not youngsters. 'What I call gentlemen villains', was the comment from one friend, 'old hands, doing about one job a year.'

ally would rather see an underworld ruled than an underworld anarchical, since it is obviously impossible to control it in any way other than from inside. Anything that tends to keep British crime British is less harmful than outside influences, at the present time: and there is nothing like being successful on your own manor to rouse enthusiasm for keeping the foreigner out. It is with the *unsuccessful* local inhabitant or the one with the chip on the shoulder who wants to boast about his friendship with the big boys, that the Transatlantic tempter makes headway. It is bad enough to have guns and ammonia. Heaven forbid that we adopt more examples from the American underworld. Give London a home team and native xenophobia has a chance to dominate the scene. It is certainly a choice of evils; but the best one can hope for is the lesser of two.

Chapter 5

THE ARCHITECTS OF ORGANISATION

The most noticeable alteration in underworld methods has been, over the years since the War, the expertise brought into the planning and execution of major crime. Unhonoured and unsung, unknown except to a few underworld characters and such of the police who remember him with dislike and a certain wry respect, the leading hero of this development was one Ernie Watts. His story is interesting to what is known among the hoods as the 'headshrinkers'; in other words, anyone who takes an interest in criminal psychology.

Ernie was the intelligent youngest child of a respectable family. The father was well known for ingenious methods in the markets, where he flogged such sundries as patent medicines of the kind beloved of gypsies; 'Bug-Fat' – popular in less hygienic days; and dustbin fly deterrents. He was insensitive to the ambitions of a son who wanted something more out of life than inherited recipes of this type and did not want to live out his days as an itinerant salesman. The child was what would now be recognised as somewhat disturbed, with over-high spirits and ensuing depression; and he was considerably spoilt by parents and doting sisters. He yearned for all the refinements of life and was ambitious.

The crisis came when he won a scholarship to Christ's Hospital. This he was not allowed to take up, despite his own pleadings and those of his headmaster; and facts support the story that he never forgot the injury or forgave life for depriving him of what he considered his real chance to better himself. He must have determined from the beginning that he was going to excel at something; and it turned out to be crime. He was not the only intelligent professional criminal I have come across: they are rare; but he had also more than the usual share of ambition, and this, ill-directed, can push a boy into strange paths. One has only to contemplate the American political scene to realise how shady practice and driving force can be intermingled on the way up: in the underworld, however, the particular driving force of true ambition is even rarer than ambition itself.

He started on small crimes while still a boy, got into minor trouble early on (which appalled his family) and then the War broke out and he duly arrived in the RAF. His record there was undistinguished (he was an unsatisfactory rather than a welcome addition) and after he parted company with the Service, he was found to be diabetic. Totting up the pros and cons of Ernie, it is fair to remember that this disease can have odd effects on personality, and could have been of long standing. Ernie, always remembered as a 'nutter', was well into the odd before he became what is known in his world as 'active'.

He began to work with two other youngsters, both of whom are alive and at the moment 'inactive'. At the time the three began working together they were young and light-hearted. Apart from the motive force of their chosen career they could have been described as nice boys – up to a point. The point was a certain latent violence. But they were larky, popular and endowed with a sense of humour which is again a rarity in a world which takes itself seriously and whose dominant emotion is suspicion. Everyone in the underworld liked them at this stage.

Ernie, like some other underworld characters, had a devoted sister who was to stand by him to the end. Her first experience of the triumvirate was when two boys unknown to her turned up for lodgings at her house with a recommendation from Ernie. They were the first, I think, to carry music-cases and describe themselves as music-students. Stories are still told about Ernie's progress, many apocryphal: what concerns us here is the fact that he applied himself with diligence to improving the professional ability of the crook and thereby permanently affected major crime. The effect that he and his boon companions had was the introduction from American crime of such elements as suited the British scene. The most important of these was a wholly new approach to planning.

Watts, apparently, had been greatly impressed by the exploits of the legendary bad baron who is supposed to have inspired Dillinger and other American gangsters. This man's history reads like a movie-script, with the villain caught out by the little man in the end. Lamm (Herman K. but always known as The Baron) had been cashiered from the German Army just before World War I, for cheating at cards. He had been a good officer and – another intellectual manqué with a chip on the shoulder – proceeded to put his talents to use as a highly successful bank-robber. He was imprisoned after a hold-up in Utah, where he had taken up residence and spent a restless time in confinement, working out how to carry out big robberies in the style of a military operation and get away with it.

His release spelt the beginning of twelve years of almost unparalleled success. For the first time, crime was planned and executed with completely military precision. He selected confederates with care. A small body of reliable ones trained for each robbery (usually a bank), every man with his own definite job and under orders to the second, as to the timing he was to observe, even if it meant leaving half the booty behind. Lamm himself was a perfectionist dictator. He was the boss and all knew it. Before each robbery he alone worked out every detail and the split-second timing which was the essence of the whole scheme. He was prone to boast that, before his gang ever entered a bank, he could draw the whole plan of it, know the method of opening every safe and accurately prophesy the reaction of every man employed therein. An old American reporter who knew him told me that Lamm's mind was remarkable both for photographic memory and ability to absorb detail. 'But', added my friend, 'he was insufferably conceited.'

Since he never took on anything but extremely profitable victims, Lamm was able to devote adequate time to each project and did so. For the first time in criminal history every detail of each projected crime was first worked out, then rehearsed again and again down to the last second, this precision being the essence of the plan. Plenty of men before and since have stolen escape cars, fast and carefully suited to the work, and many good drivers have been recruited. For Lamm, nothing but the best was good enough and even racing drivers, out of work or at loggerheads with their 'stables', were frequently bribed into driving over an escape route which had been as carefully cased for timing in all conditions as had the robbery itself. They were allowed no initiative. The timing had to be adhered to, mile by mile; not even to be speeded up, since all factors such as attracting undue attention by excessive speed at the wrong point had been taken into account. Small wonder that The Baron did well until fate, stung perhaps by excessive *hubris*, killed him off through the chance observation of a very ordinary man. A barber, who wondered why a friend was so long in the bank Lamm was robbing, strolled over with a shot gun casually under his arm to look. Lamm's luck really had run out. The driver of the escape car blew out a tyre: the gang picked up another which had had a 'governor' fixed to prevent it speeding and they finally took refuge in a lorry which had no fuel!

Readers who have studied the details of the London Airport robbery, the Great Mail Train robbery, imaginative hold-ups in two underpasses and a large collection of less publicised but equally well-cased robberies (banks and bullion in particular) will have no difficulty in recognising the pattern established by The Baron, though it is doubtful if imitators always know whose exploits inspired Ernie Watts and his associates or indeed credit Ernie himself. What their researches ensured was that crime, so often in England as amateur as everything else, began to be professional on a scale that had not previously been known. The odd thing is that Watts himself never seems to have organised anything on the gigantic scale, though he got away with a lot of profit and almost nothing in the way of convictions. There was, perhaps, an academic streak in him which enjoyed most the mental planning: not that he lacked appreciation of material achievements. It all gave him enormous psychological satisfaction. It has always been said of him that he had a crooked copper in his pocket, who actually tipped him off as to likely victims and went fifty-fifty, a story which must have *one* flaw in it at least, for I never knew a thief as generous as that.

Ernie was a strange character altogether. He could be a dedicated professional or, as one friend once said to me 'the joker of the pack'. In the middle of a serious plan involving a diamond theft, he would pause to speed across London with his friends, seeing how many smash-and-grab raids they could do in a night against a bet.[1] It is easy to see how he could inspire devotion in the amoral: many of his exploits were (and even are) quoted delightedly as being as good as *Keystone Cops*, and farcical happenings often turned up. On one occasion he led a fleeing band from the police neck-deep into a pond, but with no loss of spoils. Loaded with jewellery, on another occasion, he and the other leader fell down a lift-shaft, emerging unhurt as usual. But he, and anyone who worked with him, came out of it all well-up in the end. He is credited with many Robin Hood operations, when friends in need were helped at the expense of various department stores, but charity was not the sole purpose. Humour is something that can be thrown in, but profit is what really inspires the admiration of the underworld.

Ernie's life, in any case, was short. He died, probably by his own hand (for he had made one or two abortive suicide attempts previously) of an overdose of insulin in a London hospital; but not before he had brought to an end one friendship which had been very much a part of his life, personal and professional. The cause was the common one that he had stolen the friend's girl, whilst he was in prison. Tragedy and comedy intermingle in underworld life as elsewhere, and Ernie's deathbed provided a piece of black humour which circulated among friends and acquaintances to their great satisfaction. As he lay in the final coma, faithful colleagues – large men, well-dressed and visiting at very strange, small hours, came constantly to share his sister's vigil. One was there when the Ward Sister, bending over the bed, told them that it was all over. 'Poor chap', said the visitor, wiping away a tear. 'A good thing, otherwise we might have had to do a mercy-killing.' The nurse had no idea at all of the identity of her well-to-do, mysterious patient, and had been a little scared by and totally unable to explain the stream of strange male visitors he had had. This proved too much for her. She fled from the room to fetch reinforcements, whilst Ernie's sister, despite her grief, burst into hysterical laughter. The visitor departed, in dudgeon, deeply shocked.

[1] The answer is twelve.

The removal of Watts from the scene did not hold up progress. His associates carried on the good work and indeed improved upon it. If it seems strange that it took so long for a piece of criminal know-how to cross the Atlantic, the reason is an interesting comment upon the change that has overtaken all facets of the world in which we live. The businessman treats the world airlines today like so many bus-services. Only in the last few years has the man on the run contemplated similar commuting between such places as Mexico, Australia, Central Africa and London. The jet-set now includes the criminal as much as the company director, and both tend to travel first-class. Today, as we have seen, international co-operation in crime is a fact of everyday life: it was a prodigious novelty twenty years ago. Having observed that the up-grading of crime consequent on the highly organised 'big' job is largely due to the profits of well-organised crime, we can realise that we have not gone the length of this road yet; a long route mapped first by Ernie and his associates.

But all this is the story of what must be called the cream of the profession. The bulk of the underworld, though now respectable in outward appearance, remain psychologically the same. They continue to live much as they have always done – feckless to a degree, hand to mouth, working only when they need the money, expecting to take the rough of imprisonment with the smooth of intermittent luxury and always, Micawber-like, hopeful that something will turn up. Incurable optimists, 'one hundred per cent safe' describes every job undertaken and there are few who can resist the lure of 'Only need your car for the job' – 'Got the nightwatchman fixed – it's a piece of cake' and similar inducements. They never learn, and probably never will.

Barring the really 'good' jobs, the majority of crimes get fixed haphazardly, and are carried out quite amateurishly; which makes them more difficult to bring home in many cases. The respectable world is surrounded by ever-watchful eyes, ears always open for the dropped word which may lead to profit; it is, in short, like being in the jungle amongst predators. One gets on to their wavelength by long association: I am always aware now, when I go into a bank or shop, whether it is vulnerable or not:

I have learnt to spot the ominous absence of A or B which betokens something in the wind. When the Barclaycard first appeared I missed familiar faces and was not surprised to be told that they had been having a bash at faking – a project which fell through when it proved to be too difficult technically. There are passing crazes, when someone has a bright idea, like a wave of fake gold coins (this because 'someone' had a link with Italians until there was a quarrel): then another section will be mad on smuggling; and, of course, there is always a lookout for that hardy perennial, the long-firm fraud. But bread-and-butter crime is fairly constant and extremely dull in nature.

Mostly what happens is that someone dreams up a good idea. Perhaps a relative in office-cleaning mentions movements of valuables or notices a likely safe. A pal in furniture removals happens to talk of an interesting load, a house-painter a well-loaded 'pad',[2] or a socialite is incautious enough to be photographed in lush surroundings in a glossy magazine. A docker knows when a cargo is going by road or a lorry-driver suggests an arranged hi-jack. A bus-stop moves away from outside a jewellers, leaving the way clearer for a smash-and-grab. Many a quiet casing goes on and, as ever, there is corruption.

The idea once formed, the job is normally set up quite casually. The requisite pairs of hands are recruited, prudence keeping the numbers as low as possible for the share-out; and the plan goes on from there. Arrangements may be simple or complicated. It may be for one quick snatch or a long weekend of hot work. It may, even in simple cases, mean the renting of premises for weeks on end. There is one famous example where innocent Irish navvies worked diligently on the destruction of an internal wall adjoining a jewellers and then turned up on the Monday following the robbery to find the police in occupation, their employers fled and no wages. A spectator told me that one huge Irishman jumped up and down with rage and then hit his fellows. There are still plenty of crimes that can be done by two or three experts, even if the majority of bigger ones are now matters for

[2] Know your decorator! A complete posse of workmen left our Hampstead flat some years ago on spotting my husband who had defended one in Hertford. And I often see familiar faces in the West End, above white boiler suits!

more hands. Such is the young thief's world; and the wages are high.

Typically, all the hard work gets put in *before* the crime and there is remarkably little imagination at work as to disposal and care afterwards, which is interesting psychologically. It is as though the excitement of the crime is a sort of end in itself, a climax which obliterates the descent to everyday life. Sometimes a 'fence' is lined up first but often even this awaits events. Imagination and foresight are remarkably lacking in the underworld.

But so much is made so easy for the criminal. Newspaper offices have favourite pubs. The underworld knows and uses them all: a lot of wages go into printers' pockets and it behoves the thief to know pay-day. I have had long and entirely unfavourable gossip about myself repeated verbatim to me by a member of the underworld who happened to be eavesdropping in a Warren Street hostelry. It is not difficult to find out when wage packets are about. Bullion vans make calls: Hatton Garden is full of watching eyes, listening ears. One of the biggest bullion robberies of recent years originated in innocent but unwise discussion of time schedules. Careless talk does not belong just to wartime: it is of daily assistance to crime. So, by chance or design, in many different ways, information is collected. Time-honoured methods, already described, usually cover the robbery itself.

The high-class gang as we have seen has little difficulty in recruiting help. Since everyone wants to work with them, they can pick and choose. The small-time thief is also able to look after himself, because he will be in a position to work with just one or two friends.[8] For the medium-sized crime, everyone knows an old hand who can fix you up with the required helper, and if the helper often turns out to be a bit of a pig in a poke, well, that is life. This assistance is not quite as common as it used to be: the underworld seems to be splitting up into more specialised cells and the one-time 'fixer' nowadays is apt to be used instead

[8] Not always! I ran into a small-timer recently, sad and nostalgic. 'Saw a lovely job', he told me. 'And just couldn't get anyone to move the ladder for me and wait to put it back when I whistled. Had to give it up. Things aren't what they used to be with pals.'

to approach the Law after arrest. Allegations as to police corruption are both wildly exaggerated and understated at one and the same time. It is however my experience that a universal belief in its necessity exists in the underworld and it is obvious that a good deal of money gets 'invested' without paying any improper dividened whatever. I don't know what the moral of that is: perhaps there was substance in Lord Bacon's defence that he took bribes from both sides and decided the case according to law!

One of the constant things about crime is the way it persists in districts and particularly in those which used to be on the mail-coach routes. Though one-time slums are pulled down and high-rise, high-class flats take their place, the villains still live there in affluence as once they did in the stews; and there they talk big talk as they always did. The breweries tart-up the pubs, but everyone in the know can tell you exactly which pub in which manor remains the meeting-place for which mob. They can also tell you which to watch for particular interests. All over London, as in every provincial city, there are pubs (and clubs) in which the police meet the 'snouts' – the informers who, for a lamentably small sum compared with the wages of straightforward crime, sell their mates down the river. Most of them survive (shades of Peachum once more!) only because they are fences as well, and the same complaint is made by them, as by him, that governmental pay comes late and small. After any major crime a close interest is taken in these haunts by all concerned and by many who are not. As all the sites seem to be connected with boxing, drag or strip, it is difficult to be able to take much interest in them personally. 'The Ladies' are unwelcome. The police, one is told, prefer drag haunts as meeting-places for contacts.

As to subsequent disposal, fencing today is rarely a full-time job. Like prostitution it has suffered from enthusiastic amateurism. Stolen gold, for example, is seldom disposed of in bulk nowadays, unless it is a job fixed in advance with one of the 'rings'. A thief is lucky if, with a fence, he gets 10 per cent of the stolen value of anything he sells. 'That purchase-tax', said one, 'it's diabolical. Takes the heart out of you, it's so deceiving.' In the case of gold, if he can leak it out bit by bit, to dishonest manufacturers[4] who melt it in with their scrap in exchange for their allowance from the bullion-merchants, everyone gets a better price. With diamonds, it is much better to make arrangements out of the country: jewellery is almost always broken up. On the other hand, some major types of theft are virtually fixed by their receiver in advance,[5] as for example, art and antique robbery, which is frequently commissioned, with crook packers waiting to pack it up as something else and waft it out of the country. It is difficult to say if the old-type fence is on the way out or not and time alone will tell. He is certainly still essential to medium-class lone-type crooks.

People often ask where thieves meet to plot, though this sounds rather a grand description of the conversation centring around prospects of gain, gambling and inter-tribal gossip which makes up the small talk of the circle. When 'strictly business' is in hand and the stakes are high, they do not congregate where they are well known; but a small job does not necessarily mean secrecy, apart from the persecution mania of most of the underworld that their telephone-lines are bugged. A certain amount of unauthorised bugging does go on, despite denials of Scotland Yard, for GPO security has a high proportion of ex-policemen and, the Old Pals' Act being what it is, a keen detective sometimes exceeds his authority.[6] If this bears no fruit, no one is any the wiser; but if something interesting turns up, back-dated permission can

[4] Extremely libellous comments get made about household names in this connection. 'Biggest fences in the business' was said to me about one of our most reputable merchants!

[5] There are a number of English, as well as American 'antique dealers' in the States, particularly on the West Coast, who receive the goods. They are also useful to the fakers. The trouble is that once fakes pass into tycoon hands, no one will confess to their doubtful authenticity. 'Picassos' and 'Dufys' are acquiring pedigrees in, I think, Texas at this moment.

[6] We were ourselves sufferers from tapping during a well-known case. Whether or not this was a bit of private enterprise on the part of some police officer we were never able to discover but it was a fact that one solicitor connected with the case got a tip-off. When our line repeatedly got numbers on 'Federal' (the official private exchange), we took action. If, by the way, you have any reason to think that unauthorised bugging is going on via your telephone, it may be useful to know that a technician is attached to every exchange and no one is more keen to stop interference than the GPO.

be sought. Of course this is improper but one can well understand the reasoning. The idea that every crook's line is under supervision is complete nonsense. It is extremely difficult to get official permission for bugging and in any case there are only a limited number of available lines in Scotland Yard. These are much more frequently used for questions of national security than the pursuit of property and every hum or click does not, except to the guilty mind, suggest microphones. 'There you are! Did you hear that? Told you this line wasn't clean', frequently punctuates conversations on the blower. I often think that my line might perhaps be interesting to tap, for sheer variety, in the music-hall sense only!

A really big job does need some care in preparation. The participants will almost certainly have worked together before and will have thought out some good sites. Parks are much favoured for conferences. They are open ground and it is possible to see whether the Law is about. Each others' houses are not first favourites but most thieves have 'clean' pals whose houses can be borrowed from time to time. Clubs are apt to be risky, on account of nosey pals – female curiosity, so often spoken of, pales into insignificance beside the inquisitiveness of a thief who is not in the know and smells something in the offing. A few pubs are 'safe' and some publicans know the advantages of a small room behind the bar, though they risk their livelihood if their premises are found to be assignation points. The despised female of the species is often used as a messenger. You will find endless girls' names in underworld diaries and they are not 'dates', but the Christian names of pals' wives, useful as unofficial postwomen. They do not deceive the police for a moment.

Race-courses and dog-tracks, not to mention football crowds, are all useful, and I have heard of one mob who used to exchange confidences in the cinema: what a nuisance they must have been! They are great improvisors and any disused warehouse, railway shed or siding can get used. Caravans have been useful on occasion. There was also a legend going around that a certain combination of numbers, dialled on the phone, got you a free call,[7] and had the added advantage of getting the call through

[7] It was, I think, the code used by the engineer, testing a line.

without being picked up by any waiting listener. This was plainly nonsense but the story took a long time to die. In the event, anything goes and most things leak.

But there has been one well-kept secret. The Mail Train robbers of 1963 maintained such close security that no one else in the underworld ever had an idea of what was being hatched and this despite the fact that most people knew that something was being conceived. Like many another thing connected with this case, it is sad to contemplate so much ability, so ill directed. The underworld on the whole is almost manic-depressive in its attitude to work, bursts of furious activity alternating with idleness and inattention. The wonder is not that so few are caught, as the crime-figures suggest, but that so many escape. The ability to keep quiet and to go on planning and plotting is, fortunately for the rest of the community, rare. Few can resist that one, passing boast which undoes the work of perhaps weeks. It is not surprising that the underworld laments the imprisoned train-robbers as almost superhuman. Said one youngster to me recently, 'If they'd lived free, they say they might've done the Post Office cage.' This, the ultimate ambition of every professional thief, would make the Great Train Robbery look like peanuts. It is the strongroom, in the heart of the GPO, where *everything* of value currently in transit is stored. No one seems to know where it is, though much time and thought have been given to it. Money has been sunk, too. An old acquaintance once told me that he had bought a second-hand building-hoist, at a cost of some hundreds of pounds, in the belief that the entry could be made high up. 'No use', he said sadly. 'The chap told me quite wrong and I never even tried.'

Chapter 6

BELLMEN AND OTHERS

It is well known that some of the most fiduciary jobs in the world are not highly paid. Whatever conditions in other enterprises may be, not all security firms maintaining burglar alarms excel in generous payment or conditions for employees. These people are hard-working, often having to drive many miles in a long day for a salary that would cause dockers to strike; and these maintenance men are those who, if they can be tempted to 'go crook' when they change jobs, are the most valued allies of the thief. Not many do; but it is from among the ranks of such firms that the best bellmen have been drawn – and for these obvious reasons.

The bellman today must know a good deal more than the mere silencing of alarm systems and he must be prepared to work in with a team, advancing step by step along the circuits as the break-in proceeds. He must understand the working of a thermic lance (the 'laser' of thrillers) and although this is often said to be old-hat and something that everybody knows how to work, it is not true. A thermic lance is always an awkward object to handle, and is only employed when time-honoured methods are unsuitable, being extremely hot, producing a lot of smoke of a choking variety and a lot of noise too.[1] It requires experience to handle it, especially as it can 'blow back' in unskilled hands and kill the operator who fails to escape. It is not at all suitable for all premises, but it may be necessary when thick walls have to be pierced quickly and is often used if time is short, metal melting and concrete crumbling to powder before it. The bellman does not intrude on the duties of a 'peterman' or safe opener, but must

[1] The taped conversations which were mentioned in connection with the Lloyds Bank robbery at Baker Street were full of complaints about the effects of the lance. 'My eyes feel like they were on stalks – all bunged up.' 'The smoke's terrible – you can't breathe', etc.

usually stand by even when the door is opened, in case, if the lance or gelignite does not work out, his skills may be required again to attack from another angle. As the most worthwhile premises are now guarded in triplicate at times, the bellman's job is increasingly dangerous and requires more skill than ever: result – it is even more highly paid. The temptation is strong to a man, near retiring age on the meagre pay of an honest life, when the rich freelance fee is offered him by a top gang. What he does not realise in most cases is that this is no one-off job; he will be blackmailed for the rest of his life.

Some knowledgeable bellmen still fight shy of going on the job, and not surprisingly. They prefer to give advice from a distance and will perhaps coach likely apprentices and, unless things are very complicated, this is often a welcome arrangement. A well-dressed, middle-aged professional may be advised to make a call on a safe-firm, his card specially printed for the occasion suggesting that he is connected with a substantial company. He will talk about the latest advances in the protection of premises with the firm; and a lot can be learned that way. A good bellman anyway can teach, at remote control, how to immobilise a particular site. (One such man did so in the real crime considered in Chapter 2.) Sometimes the bellman is acquainted with the actual premises concerned and can warn about 'tremblers' which go off with vibration, or advise the use of planks across floors which are protected but give no audible or visual warning of the fact. In any case he will take or plan precautions. Except for the super specialist the majority of bellmen come from within the underworld itself and have usually been successful burglars. In becoming specialists themselves they work rather harder than they used to. One, recently at large again, has diligently attended night-school, worked in a well-known firm between 'jobs' and actually been a security repair man. He is not much liked among professional colleagues as he is not above 'shopping' pals on occasion; but there are few really big snatches of recent years that have not had the benefit of his advice, though he makes it a condition of employment that he is paid first and is well away before any of the gang actually enter the premises: his recent imprisonment was for something else. 'Well-respected' is the verdict; but he is not popular in the clubs. He sits in a favourite seat in his customary pub, drinking with the cousin who works the thermic lances (and therefore has to be well paid also, since he doubles for the maestro if anything else in the alarm system requires attention) but he usually drinks with no one else. He is said to have made enough to retire on. Few underworld characters would ever admit to such a situation but if he did not bet so much, the report might even be true in his case.

There are a lot of bellmen about. Their skills vary and so does their status. A gang likes to have its 'regular' unless some super specialist is required and education and the acquiring of electrical and electronic knowledge (usually at the taxpayers' expense) have made many a skilful operator. The one hope for the forces of law and order is that, at this moment, science seems to be keeping one small jump ahead of crime and the latest electronic devices on the most worthwhile premises (such as the assayers), are, on the whole (and at great expense) a bit beyond most of the bellmen. These safeguards are only on a few sites so far, and they are extremely expensive to install. Other premises and strong rooms respond to orthodox and violent methods. Ordinary safes, unless there is a key and/or a combination at hand, can be opened with gelignite, muffling the explosion adequately and setting it off by the assembly of the detonator which will fire it. 'Jelly' is simple to procure. Some comes from Army stores, as does a lot of ammunition, stolen or illegally procured. But jelly mostly comes from Scottish mines and is sold openly in the bar of a certain Glasgow pub. *Vidor* is their favourite make of reliable battery and nothing will persuade them that take-overs have equalised quality.

The underworld soon learn, from experience or the teaching of others, to spot the safe which looks well-protected but is assailable from the back; and once more the surprise is how many firms will economise and lose. As safes get better – and they can be highly sophisticated today – a very different situation arises. Where a small impregnable safe is concerned, the orthodox method is to remove it *in toto*: it is useless if you have coveted jewellery to put your trust in the little strongbox hidden in the wall or under the floorboard. Above all, it is vital to know your installer, for the thieves know many. Determined thieves will work for months to find a clue to the code which will open a strongroom or safe where really big money is involved, and will place an ally amongst cleaners or even temporary clerical staff to find out any scraps of necessary information or to take a wax or soap impression, if any superior is careless with keys: there are many who are. Peterman and associates will watch the comings and goings of the nightwatchman, possibly chatting him up in his 'local': incorruptible or non-forthcoming he may be, but unless he is suspicious at least his routine can be learned. If the honest were not so often creatures of habit, the way of the transgressor would be made much more difficult.

The stoppo-driver is another highly-rated villain. Like the bell-man, he is almost invariably a regular member of the operating gang: there are a few free-lances, one of them being a woman (which shows rare trust indeed in the underworld, who have a Victorian approach to feminine assistance); but one hears criticisms. These stoppo boys have really got to drive well and know the meaning of punctuality. The only minicab business that I ever found reliable was one operated by underworld staff, which I used for a time in the belief that this was helping ex-prisoners in honest work. There was one thing about this firm you could rely on and that was timing. As by subsequent report the firm could produce, at the drop of a hat (or, to be more accurate, the call of a phone) the driver for any smash-and-grab raid whose regular had let them down, this was natural. It is a pity not to be able to recommend it to busy people who would appreciate this particular virtue but it is out of business – naturally also, and for a long time to come. They had one driver who never lacked initiative. I was once being driven by him through Brewer Street, in heavy traffic, when behind us sounded the bell of an accident ambulance. Without a moment's hesitation L mounted the *double* kerb stone, sped along the footway and dropped down again, pursued by the ambulance. There was a young constable on duty at the corner. 'That was naughty of you, sir', he said, 'but thank you all the same. It was sensible in the circumstances – and a good bit of driving.' L looked at me with a seraphic smile as we drove off. 'He's young, isn't he?', he said. 'He doesn't know my ugly mug and he doesn't know who drove the escape-car last

Wednesday.' It is not 'done' to ask questions where knowledge is incriminating but last Wednesday must have meant a largeish job; L never works except for the 'best'. He is a great snob.

The drivers are also people whose cars never seem to get removed by the police. Accustomed to stealing cars, they are expert at immobilising transport or at least making it so difficult that, human nature being what it is, their cars get left much longer than anyone else's. There was a day when, after a legal conference which went on rather longer than usual and involved a view of premises where the offence had been committed, learned Counsel came out to find that all their cars had been removed to the police pound for parking offences and were grateful for a lift there from the client in the case. As the underworld is prone to remark, with quite a different meaning, 'There is no justice in the world'.

Warren Street, that fertile source of information, is the stamping-ground of most stoppos. Those who worked with mail-horses in the old days were handy with their tip-offs to the highwaymen[2] and today, when the honest car-dealer lives surrounded by car-thieves, ringers and hire-purchase swindlers, the Street offers exciting prospects for speed-mad juveniles who can match-up to underworld specifications. Many are called and few chosen, for a gang is literally putting its lives in the hands of an escape-driver and there is no sentiment to spare for a slip-up. Moreover, escape driving involves much more than mere speed. The escape-driver must do a lot of preliminary homework. If a big load, for instance, is involved, the double-back tactic may be involved. This means, roughly, that if a chase begins, the driver must know the prearranged point on the motorway or other road where he can slip into another waiting car just inside an off-turning and, abandoning the first, drive in the opposite direction, sometimes even passing the pursuing police with his load. The manœuvre may be repeated several times and a skilful gang with a really big haul makes deliberate use of this method, planning in advance so that any pursuit will be confused, cars for changing being

[2] Says Mat o' the Mint in *The Beggar's Opera*, 'I drink a dram now and then with the stage-coachman in the way of friendship and intelligence and I know that about this time there will be passengers upon the western road who are worth speaking about.'

strategically placed along the route with new drivers, and even changes of outer clothing. This accounts for some of the incomprehensible places in which stolen cars are sometimes found (most escape cars have been carefully selected and stolen for the job) and, as can be seen, the careful planning that has to be done in advance means a responsible attitude which goes far beyond show-off driving, though we are talking of top-class gang work when so much preparation has been done. The risk in employing amateurs or semi-amateurs is that they are not always prepared to do their homework.

Apprenticeship to crime means, amongst other things knowing all the 'Burglars' Routes' – the small roads, yet allowing for reasonable speed, which an escape-car can take to avoid traffic or road-blocks: roads which have frequently on them small sanctuaries in case of need – a garage here, a tall hedge there, a warehouse with a key to the door. No well-trained thief in his senses uses a motorway or main road that can be blocked, except to gain distance before the alarm is given. An experienced, seasoned driver must be able to keep cool, to be able to bluff his way out. Bowler hats are about played out. But recently a Bentley, driven by a neatly uniformed chauffeur and bearing the House of Lords insignia, went through a road-block with 'Milord' in the back holding a briefcase which contained stolen jewellery. The badge was a forgery: the Bentley had been 'borrowed' – whatever that may mean. I still think that 'College Harry', running in his underpants through several cordons of police and posing as an enthusiastic athlete holds the laurel against his mechanised juniors!

There are a certain number of quieter drivers, of mature experience, who work almost locally. One gang used to specialise in quick robberies with a driver who could thread his way through any maze of streets to Kensal Green where, in a secluded part of the cemetry, rearrangements could be made and other cars assemble for the small share-out. This again, I believe, was used in some film or TV play or other, in complete innocence. Truth and fiction do sometimes meet. Today the work of the driver, lurking round the corner from the victim's premises or circling to await the prearranged signal has been made much harder by the cruising around of the hated Panda car. Less and less can be left to chance and more and more has to depend on inside information, so that the wages can be snatched at the exact time of their return from the bank or the van raided at a known and anticipated call. Then indeed a driver will show his skill – and God help anyone who gets in his way.

The natural auxiliary to any gang who needs an escape-car is a 'heister'. By this method the young thief often proves his worth and if he falls down on the job, he is easily dispensable and will probably not 'shop' – or be able to shop – anyone of much consequence. Car-stealing is not as difficult as it ought to be. The great majority of vehicles are not well protected: like house or flat premises, to delay the thief is the great safeguard, since it is almost impossible to protect private property, moveable or immoveable, against the determined thief; but it is possible to make things difficult enough to turn his attention elsewhere. Many a wife knows how often her husband leaves the car unlocked: many alleged safety devices are not worth having. A thief who is stealing for a job knows exactly what car he is going for – Jaguars are often preferred since they are fast and not so uncommon as to attract attention; and any good, ordinary coloured family saloon is useful and therefore risks being stolen for short runs, perhaps from the site of a robbery to another car, a ruse to confuse pursuers. If one could bear it, a high-powered car would be rather well protected by psychedelic colouring! The heister will in any case be equipped with all the keys he needs and will also be expert in all the dodges for starting a car without them. The biter sometimes gets bit. One who has stolen and driven hundreds of other people's cars in his day was righteously indignant when his own was 'done' during lunch. An invention which punctured a tyre just about five minutes after unlawful removal would be useful to prevent theft; for a quick flip round the nearest corner, or, if everything is planned to that schedule, to the garage 'in' on the job, a change of number-plates and the thief is away.

Stealing to sell is another matter. This is quite a different operation and involves complete 'ringing' with change of number-plates, colour, engine-numbers and so forth, with the collaboration of a dishonest garage being almost inevitable. Not that everybody knows that windows and windscreens undo thieves who are too lazy to carry out a thorough job. If you look at your own car, you will find a code-number on them, which corresponds roughly to the date when they were made. Disparity between these and the altered log-book or engine-number is one of the leads police look for when they are tracing stolen cars. The immense number that disappear each day is easily noticed by listening to the police radio on VHF – the most popular programme of the underworld.

Always one comes back to the hereditary and the traditional in crime. The car-thief's ancestors most likely stole horses; the lorry hi-jacker is the lineal descendant of the canal-boat robber, who lifted the load at the lock-keeper's cottage by arrangement or otherwise. The handbag-snatcher is our old friend the footpad; the little man who hangs about telephone booths for the gloves, umbrellas and briefcases that callers seem to leave so frequently for a moment or two before they realise their loss, is in direct descent from the sneak-thief who used to pop into the mail-coach as the passengers descended and do a quick theft. The Great Mail Train robbers were, after all, just highwaymen – one or two have looked a bit rueful as I remarked that they would have made a pretty picture in the cart to Tyburn. When gambling was at its most prosperous, there were good pickings to be had by following winning gentlemen to a quiet spot: Gay makes one of Macheath's gang remark on the benefits to be had when gaming had been good in the Marylebone gaming houses – and it is not so far from one of the largest today.

Con-men are not much liked in the underworld and they are extremely unpopular in prison.[3] After all, in an atmosphere of general suspicion, this is reasonable. Exploits are admired and often quoted, but there is an uneasy feeling amongst the acquaintances that he who sups with them should use a sufficiently long spoon. Occasionally one feels a certain sympathy for them when they remove ill-gotten gains from victims. On the whole I concur in disliking them, though there are exceptions. My least favourite

[3] Oddly enough, this is often endearing to the public! Anything for a laugh, I suppose.

inhabitant of the underworld is neither murderer, blackmailer nor rapist but a con-man; a view shared by most of those who know him. It is really remarkable that he has survived so long. There will be no tears shed when he comes to a sticky end, but the English underworld is really remarkably tolerant.

There is of course a lighter side to con-men. Delighted raconteurs will tell you of S who married three wives, all for their money, kept friends through the divorces and managed recently to run up a startling overdraft on the third's bank account. Charm is his stock-in-trade and he is a most efficient worker, who learnt his business through Australian tuition. But conning is essentially a cruel game, worse than normal theft. It is rotten for any citizen to come home and find that he has been burgled and no one can suggest that thieves are sensitive to other people's feelings, but it feels even worse when someone has wriggled himself into the confidence of a trusting soul and then fleeced the victim bare. Recently a man's whole life-savings were stolen from him in this way: he is sixty-odd, ill, and with a sister to look after. One of my older acquaintances, A, normally (like most of his colleagues) prudish, insensitive about robbing people, and careful of his language in front of ladies, is of the same opinion. 'Now the straight grafter', he said, one afternoon, 'You know where you are with him. Maybe you've been on a job or two or you know he's spoke well of – but this load of muck we're talking of, there's only one word for him and I don't like to use it. Arsel-creeper, that's what he is and I hope you don't mind me saying it.' Anglo-Saxon ruderies are rare in the underworld, which mostly uses rhyming slang or gypsy expressions and I was interested to hear this survival in use. What is more, it was a piece of accurate character assessment that could not be bettered. (I have met it since. In this case it was applied in prison to the successful applicants for parole by the less lucky ones.) It is *the* greatest word of condemnation in underworld parlance. Obviously there is an absolute rottenness on which the two worlds can agree.

The underworld is not so much black as grey. The grey can merge into sinister darkness but a high proportion of criminal conduct is just pettily shabby. What hits the headlines is violence, lust and guns: attendance at any magistrate's court gives a truer picture of the whole, as the dreary little *vignettes* of life below the line are drawn. So, when the indignant thief berates the con-man who has betrayed a pal and suggests that he should be put up against the wall and shot, his indignation is as genuine as that of 'Disgusted' of Wimbledon, who would like the drug-addict horsewhipped. But perhaps 'Disgusted' would carry out the sentence. The genuinely indignant criminal, when it comes to the point, would not even 'shop' the con-man.

There are other aspects of 'conning' crimes such as fraud, but it might be as well to consider what crimes are 'down' at the moment and what is virtually non-existent on the British scene. Kidnapping, so far, seems to be a non-British activity – and long may it remain so. The horrifying McKay case[4] was not underworld work, though many people have held their breath lest it might put ideas into heads. Gangs in the American sense are also almost non-existent, though with violence so widespread, one might be forgiven for confusing it. The Kray and Richardson experiments in gangster-type operation might have started something if they had been successful: their failure to 'jell', in the end and (for once!) a salutary effect from long sentences has had the effect of cooling enthusiasm for this sort of alliance of 'gangster' and hired man,[5] though nothing, as remarked before, will ever stamp out small-scale blackmail.

The 'gang' who will carry out a big well-planned raid – a bank vault, a West End jewellers, a bullion van or the like – are not the 'gangsters' whose in-fighting makes occasional headlines in the Press. 'Gang Warfare – Gangland Killing – Terror Gang Strikes Again – Murdered Man Thought to be Victim of Gangland Revenge' – refer to something far removed from the operators who team up to carry out a big robbery. Gangland in-fighting is virtually confined to the moronic no-goods who are recruited as dispensable hands for the purpose of doing day-to-

[4] Mrs McKay, wife of a newspaper man, was kidnapped by mistake for the wife of Mr Rupert Murdoch, the proprietor of the *News of the World*, the *Sun* and some Australian newpapers. No trace of her was ever found but evidence pointed to her murder by two brothers named Hussein, who were arrested and convicted for the offence. See also Chapter 11.

[5] As I write, a swift police swoop has been made on a smaller attempt to set up a protection racket.

day crime (largely on commission) for criminal hirers who have no intention of doing jobs themselves, but who have ordinary thefts as a bread-and-butter sideline as well as larger rackets, like protection. A lot of little people are also 'fronts' for such operations as long-firm frauds: sometimes they work as small-time burglars and general 'grafters' and are hired for a well-set-up robbery, such as lorry hi-jacking. It is rare for intelligent underworld characters to have anything to do with well-known gangsters of this type, except when they want some dirty work done – this is not unknown. As may be imagined, the hired dim-wits often try their hands at cheating their hirers, with the result that punishment gets meted out. Since the whole picture of this segment of the underworld life is one of low mentality and consequent violence, mayhem and murder are apt to be the rule and the cruelty and bestial violence that ensue are as bad as anything to be found in the underworld. Just once in a while, a 'better-class' thief gets embroiled, but this is rare. As for the victims, they are of all too dispensable a category and their disappearance is not always noticed. 'The wells behind Brighton want draining', said one woman to me.

Gang rows of an internecine type always exist, but they do not often impinge on respectable people and so far at least, this country has been spared the American spectacle of the police, in pursuit of gangster-robbers, shooting far more innocent spectators than thieves. Where violence is concerned, the general toleration of gun-carrying by the younger generation is far the most disquieting factor in the situation. Yet even here, with world-wide violence nudging one's consciousness all the time, it is worth remembering that we are nowhere near the situation of the nineteenth century when few streets were safe.

Race-course gangs are on the wane, though they have expanded on doping (corruption almost always). The bookmakers would not like a remark made by a most experienced racing enthusiast (illegal); 'If you made all betting on the Tote, you could cut out doping tomorrow.' Here is one field in which 'respectable' and 'unrespectable' meet and mingle so closely that each takes the other's colour. I never knew any play take underworld fancy like *The Jockey Club Stakes* in which crooks and Establishment figures rival one another in skullduggery. Who can prevent a thirsty horse having a nice drink of pure water at the wrong moment, as many a bribed stable-boy could say? As for medical doping, this is a matter in which each side tries to keep one trick ahead of the other.

Bigamy has vanished: marriage-lines are not valued as they were. Prostitution has completely altered and so has pimping, both hampered by amateurs; and a lot of profitable blackmail has gone owing to the healthier attitude to homosexuality, its oldtime basis. Coining, except for gold antiques, is much less. There is not much that is worth it today and the silver coins that used to be made from soda-siphon tops have vanished with the plastic replacements and the florins themselves: a few underworld wives worked away at polishing up old halfpennies for new 2p pieces – but such peanuts were not worth it. I own a very nice but peeling 'gold' five-pound piece which was the dummy-run of a major effort which did not come off. I have not heard of much recently but no doubt it will recur. The Italians are the best fakers, and forgery, though always with us to some extent, is not what it was. Cheque books are stolen and cheques are still forged by many but stolen credit cards are easier and quicker. Great admiration for massive operations in America on forged credit cards has not as yet produced worthwhile imitations here. But it is unwise to prophesy about the underworld. As likely as not, an almighty forgery will break on the world as this book goes to press. There is no reason why it should not.

Chapter 7

THE FEMALE TOUCH

Few women in this country get involved in crimes other than shoplifting, which can be a deliberate way of earning a living, or some sort of kick, usually the result of emotional stress, often at the menopause. If they do they are generally there because of a man; a husband, a boyfriend, sometimes a brother. The lot of an underworld wife is a sorry one. Of course she spends the money when it is there, and knows where it comes from: in similar circumstances, it takes a good deal of imagination to believe that most of us would do anything else, if it were the only available housekeeping. Some wives desert; but remarkably few. At the back of many underworld marriages is the pathetic and oft-repeated story of the girl who thought she could reform him: others have been carried away by the attractions of the boy who was 'different', the boy who had always got the money for the exciting outings which the steady boyfriend could not provide. Things seldom go according to her plan. The dream fades. The girl becomes a nervy, worn-out woman who jumps at every ring of the doorbell, waking early in the morning after the experience of too many 6 a.m. knocks on the door, accompanied by the call to 'Open up!'

On the whole these girls stand by their men. They try to cover up for them, to hide stolen goods in the airing-cupboard or behind the sink, and then lie their heads off to the police; or they cook up impossible alibis which often sink the men effectively. They tell the children tales, which can have traumatic effects, to conceal the truth about their fathers: sometimes they confide in the kids and take them along on prison visits and I know of few sadder sights than the waiting rooms of the various nicks. There sit the wives, in the trendiest clothes they can find, from minimal skirts to outrageous pants-suits; make-up fiercely worn, like a flag, with the children dressed to kill. You see them all afterwards, weeping and deflated. I often travel on the Isle of Wight boat with them after a Parkhurst visit, and they need a stiff brandy before the brave front comes on again. It is not easy to go back to live with the neighbours' talk. School and school friends are not always kind to prisoners' children; and when the father comes home, it is often just an interval before something that has to be gone through all over again. Glamour and excitement may exist for the man in a criminal career, but seldom does the wife of a recidivist see much of it. Many of these women are in the underworld but not necessarily of it. Among them are a number of fiercely honest ones, who have to work hard, long hours to provide the family with the means to live; concealing their identities wherever possible and terrified of Press intrusion after a 'big job'. In the end most of them give up the struggle and just go with the tide. Their friends become the husband's friends, often the wives of his mates, in a circle where at least there is nothing to conceal. Eventually crime and everything to do with it becomes the ordinary fabric of life and, like sickness or unemployment, it just has to be endured. A callus grows over the wound and nothing hurts so much again.

But by no means all underworld wives are tragic figures. Success in crime, no less than in any other occupation, brings material advantages and the well-heeled wife is very well-heeled indeed. To be the wife of a top thief, however, brings with it other complications, such as husbandly nervousness about the proceeds of successful robberies while he is in prison, either through boyfriends with fortune-hunting in mind or the ever-present danger of the con-man; and the number of domestic break-ups is much higher here than in the case of those women who are not doing very well out of crime. It is easy enough to condemn some of these more authentic 'Moll' figures, but there is still quite a difference between women who only assist in a fairly passive capacity and the very small band of women who play an active role in the underworld in their own right.

Thirty years ago, if you excluded shoplifters (always liable to be unbalanced personalities though also including hard-headed go-getters) there were practically none. From time to time a woman might be picked up as an accessory to a crime; now and then there would be the odd escape-driver, always described by Press as blonde, and beautiful by implication: a view which does not correspond with my own recollections of these rare birds (in every sense of the word). If caught, they seldom return to crime. However unsuitable prison may be for women it really does seem to discourage quite a lot of them. But in the past twenty years there have been just one or two who have achieved notoriety in underworld circles at least. The most interesting is a particularly intelligent and handsome woman who drifted into it all by accident: once in it she took to it like the proverbial duck to water, finding there an outlet for her exuberant vitality and her perpetual longing for adventure.

If she could tell her tale it would be a fascinating and accurate account of major crime over the last twenty years, but it is impossible to envisage anyone publishing it since it would involve every name of note in the underworld – and not only in Britain. How often she has actually 'been on the job' is anyone's guess (she certainly describes vividly the tensions inside locked and darkened premises as a robbery proceeds with a photographic detail which suggests the participant rather than someone who has heard it at second-hand). She has been well known as a willing and accomplished assistant and succourer on many major occasions and is one of the most trusted people in her own world. If no one else has accurate information about some sudden crime, she will know it within minutes: professional pride is at stake and she will dig down to discover whatever is not immediately clear to her. The reason for her success is probably that she has the tightest mouth in the underworld; nothing and nobody can drag out of her anything she does not intend to tell, though she confesses to great fear of police interrogation. This sounds like admiration on my part. It is, in fact, merely respect for a remarkable personality. In a world where people are not trustworthy, she is: in a man's world, she has made woman admired as man's equal (and sometimes superior) and, although the ethics to which she holds are not those of our world, she has kept steadfastly to her own and often to her disadvantage. As with some other intelligent characters one's feeling is 'what a waste of good human material'.

She soon became a citizen of the world like her associates: today, there are few more reliable guides to the jet-routes, their virtues and foibles. With an excellent sense of humour and the ability not to take herself seriously, she is unlike most of the underworld. Dogged by ill-health and with more than her share of domestic troubles, she keeps that side of things to herself, and remains ironically cheerful. Children are her passion: she cares more than the majority of 'respectable' people for what can become of children, because she has had plenty of experience of what happens in the darker world in which she lives. Cruelty and violence she openly abhors: there is some inconsistency here, for her associates do not share her views when they get in the way of business: for honesty, she cares not a jot, and glories in successful crime, which must, however, be skilled to excite her admiration. G. K. Chesterton would have liked to know her, for she is emphatically not 'the joyless sinner who sins without reward' and it is doubtful if he ever met so concrete an example of something he was always longing to encounter in real life. How to assess Kate is a puzzle. She has courage, principles, kindliness and loyalties – and is a thorough nuisance to society. If any assessment at all can be made, it means evaluating the whole question of the relative gravity of crimes. Is dishonesty something to make the angels weep, as distinct from landing the doer in the dock? Can you compare it (as Judges have to do every day) with violence, cruelty, wanton disregard for human relationships—dishonesty, in itself, being a fairly wanton disregard of other people's rights? Among those whose standards differ so profoundly from ours I find it impossible to form firm judgements. Uncertainty, plus the realisation of one's inadequacy in this respect does kick one, out of sheer cussedness, into greater personal honesty, possibly in self-defence. Kate refuses to comment on this. But she stoutly maintains her principles. No writer of indignant letters to *The Times* on juvenile delinquency and violence, particularly the carrying of guns, can make a more powerful indictment; and she does not hold her tongue on it. She has good reason to know what is happening. 'I shall end in the Thames,' she said to me once and was not joking. She had spoken her mind to a dangerous thug and was realising the risks.

The position of women in the underworld has always been that of second-class citizens. The swaggering male (in success) and the deflated failure (in defeat) are both well known to wife and mother. It takes a major crisis indeed to make a member of the underworld admit that he is, as in fact he so often is, dependent upon woman's loyalty for life and liberty. Kate's position is an unusual one:[1] she is commonly known there as 'Ma Barker', though the comparison to that odious character is unjust and inaccurate.

It was through being a fanatical Baptist when young that she started on her present way of life. Ironically when a brother got into trouble and needed help the way to crime opened. 'More compelling than a husband,' she says. His associates were attractive and their activities were fun. Gradually it was accepted that a woman could and would be the one to come and pick them up when they were stranded; and eventually when they were not. One of the most difficult driving jobs is that of dropping the burglar off at an appointed time and then picking him up again at exactly the right moment – and without attracting suspicion; and this happened to fit a good woman driver rather well. Not too difficult in a busy town: nerve-racking in a country lane, with country eyes liable to be upon you. Women can, as one thief grudgingly admitted 'use their loaf'.[2]

Having learnt the 'Burglars' Routes' across London and adding some refinements, she became expert at moving 'gear', intelligence and the ability to talk herself out of a situation standing her in good stead. These were the days of the big cigarette hijackings. She once fooled the police with a haul of a million or so of these, by the mere chance that her own packet (the same brand) could be accounted for in a local shop. 'But I sweated for days,' she said. 'That load was hidden too near for comfort.' It was.

[1] Ma Barker (also a Kate) presided over the worst of the gangs of the Dillinger days. Curiously enough, she, like Kate, began with a taste for religion, especially revival meetings. There the resemblance ends. Ma was a great one for murder and revelled in sadistic detail.

[2] 'Loaf' is one of the bits of Cockney rhyming slang which lives on in ordinary speech. Loaf of bread – head.

It was in a nearby shed. Once there was a trip to Newbury, in answer to a midnight call for help, to pick up on foot a 'passenger'. This was the fugitive from an unsuccessful raid on a house. He appeared, early the next morning, having attached himself inconspicuously to the last rank of a column of just recruited soldiers – without *his* 'gear'. Rescue took many forms, as when the rescued turned up in his socks, his shoes lost in a muddy field as he fled. Things do not always go smoothly for the thief. There was a night when it was necessary to get into a sleeping-car, whilst the train was in the sheds, awaiting the cleaner, to find, in a few moments, £50,000 worth of jewellery hidden under a bunk. This she successfully accomplished; though she blenched on the occasion when asked to go and pick up the spoils from a broken-down car, which turned out to be full of stolen 'one-armed bandits', then selling for £100 each. 'Burglars' cars' she remarked, 'seem even more liable to breakdown than are those of the honest'; but of course in most cases they are the cars of the honest, stolen and over-driven for the occasion; and the nursing of a faltering car and the quick change to another and yet another in one night was all part of her job.

Are women going to be liberated into crime? The barrier, up till now, has been male unwillingness to accept any active feminine co-operation, women being regarded merely as confidante, cover-up and 'drop'. At the moment it looks unlikely that women will get into the last bastion of the underworld. The clubs sacred to the fraternity are more sex-biased than the Stock Exchange and few underworld wives or girlfriends really match up to the life involved. But teenage girls are beginning to get into mischief with their boys; and it looks like the thin end of the wedge. One girl was recently involved actively in a bank raid. It may be the advance of liberation: it has on occasion had links with drugs. It was unheard of until recently and the 'squares' of the mature underworld regard it with horror.

Another development springs to mind. Is Myra Hindley unique? Mary Bell, convicted at eleven for the killing of two three-year-old boys 'for pleasure' is the first child murderer, so far as I know, in England[3] (since the monstrous offspring of Sawney

[3] Another is being charged at the time of writing.

Bean, all of whom are reported to have been extremely partial to murder, preceding cannibalism). The only woman murderer working with a gang whom I have met personally was a citizen of Holland, though herself a Belgian. She had been one of a group of successful bank-robbers and had joined it to work with her lover and his associates. In the end, an unsuccessful attempt on a bank led to the shooting of a policeman, whose body the robbers tried to stuff into the boot of their car. It was Marie who suggested that it would be easier to do if they chopped the protruding legs off – and helped to do so! She was working in the prison laundry when I met her, completely unrepentant, bored with prison uniform and routine (in that order), a good-looking woman who had outworn her romance with the robber lover and had no intention of getting into prison again. This decision was not made on any moral grounds but because it was not sensible and she did not like prison. It was more profitable to go into horticulture and she had planned to do so.

What was rather frightening about this good-looking and charming woman who had managed, in prison, to create a good hair-do for herself and other prisoners; and to press prison gingham into a tidy, not unbecoming working uniform, was her complete ordinariness. She might have been a skilled laboratory technician showing a chance visitor round the works and making pleasant conversation on the way. She was ready to discuss her previous life, without embarrassment or excitement. It had been a job and that was all there was to it. It had turned out to be an unprofitable job: the lover had not come up to scratch and she could easily find another, the shrug of the shoulders suggested. Quite at ease, her attitude was different from the normal masculine one, where, when questioned in this way, there is a tendency either to be slightly embarrassed or to go in for a bit of chest-beating to impress the listener. One did not feel that Marie was in the least what used to be called a 'moral imbecile': she is possibly schizophrenic, as are so many prison inhabitants; but she is not quite like these people either. She had made up her mind to keep out of crime and was clearly going to do so but the motive was as amoral as the crime itself. If Marie is the blueprint of a new type of woman offender, the prospect is formidable. Women know that women in a man's world have to be some fifty per cent better at their job than a man, to stand up to the competition: the thought of Marie's cold efficiency, linked to Kate's intelligence and stoical qualities makes the blood run cold. There have been a few American cases of women involved with men in crimes, as in a macabre rape and murder case in Lansing, near Ypsilanti: a couple were also arrested in England in 1969 for sexual offences against girls, committed by a middle-aged man and a young girl. But the English case was in no way connected with the underworld proper (where sex offences are very unpopular indeed): so far, we have not bred Marie and the first all-woman gang. I hope this happy state continues.

Chapter 8

CREEPING CORRUPTION

Whoever wrote the well-known hymn:

> 'Christian dost thou feel them,
> How they work within,
> Striving, tempting, luring,
> Goading into sin.'

must have been thinking of the underworld. Corruption has already been mentioned in connection with specific activities, but it crops up again and again and is worth consideration in more detail, for it plays so large a part in underworld life. Supreme opportunists, most villains are always hopeful that a short cut will be available if only the right person can be suborned – and he often is.

Corruption has many faces and is not all on one side. There is the ever-present attempt to square the police. This endeavour has always gone on and the older generation of crooks asserts that, contrary to the usual belief, it is not so bad in its effects as it used to be. It appears still to be customary among the 'pros' to offer something as soon as the victim is nicked. In many districts there is a regular tariff – so much for the Inspector, so much for the Sergeant. This potentially libellous statement needs explanation.

Corruption which actually affects the course of justice in any way is not widespread in the police. It occurs patchily and everyone in the underworld knows where these patches exist. The man on the beat (or in the Panda as he is mostly today) is not as vulnerable as the CID: the Flying Squad are exposed to the highest pressure by the very nature of their work. It is unfortunate for everyone that maximum publicity is always given to a slip-up here and that maximum harm probably ensues. News is news. A straight copper generally becomes news only when he is the victim of a shooting. The fact that money is offered does not necessarily mean its acceptance: there are plenty of instances where the 'fixer' (the underworld character who is 'in' with the law and does the dirty work) has nicked the lot whilst averring that the law has done everyone down. But a lot of money does change hands. There must be a number of men in the police force who observe the policy of Bacon already mentioned, who maintained that he took bribes from both sides and decided the case according to its merits. (This might not be a bad thing, I have often thought. It ought to teach the bribers quicker than anything else.) Once in a way, however a bribe alters the course of justice. Quite helpless to do anything about it, I am aware at the moment of a case of unequal sentencing, due to this, which has embittered at least one prisoner of whose subsequent reform there could be hopes, to the point where it is impossible to make him believe that justice is straight or that it is worth while trying to go straight himself. Even to know of one case of this sort is shocking; but it is not unique.

Most money that is accepted merely goes into a convenient police pocket and is lost to the briber. It is always paid in cash and usually to a relative, leaving no trace. It is not a pleasant thought but it is not nearly so unpalatable or so serious as the blackmail tactics occasionally used in reverse, when a prisoner or his wife is approached by the police with a demand for money or else.

Police blackmail never seems to be tried except in the case of a man with a thoroughly bad record, which makes it worse, as he is then in a hopeless position. It *does* happen – not nearly as often as the underworld would have you believe, allegations of this sort being more or less standard; and again this is another field in which the old boys of the underworld maintain things have improved. Time was, they say, when the planting of gelignite or housebreaking implements, etc. was done on a regular rota, more or less as the prostitutes used to be rounded up in rotation. It no longer happens like this but the modern version, demanding much larger sums of money in return for not pressing a charge hard, is certainly in existence. However, the matter can be exaggerated: once more it should be said that it occurs in localised patches only and it is, by general (and for once accurate) report, confined to larger cities.

Another serious aspect of corruption is the bent policeman who tips off the crook. Sometimes the bending is voluntary and profitable. But sometimes the policeman is blackmailed into co-operation. The great old trick (which works with prison-officers as well) is to get the victim to slip-up, just once and on quite a small thing. Then you have got him. It used to be done frequently around Soho. It was just too easy to give a 'present' – perhaps even a birthday party to the wife who was out for the night with her husband – with some small favour of a harmless nature – more or less – asked for in return, not necessarily at the time; something so small that an officer, who had perhaps had a drop more of the hard stuff than he was used to, would agree to before he realised what he was in for. There was a case years ago which illustrates the point. A young officer was induced to keep a criminal record out of the file for just twenty-four hours – easily done in the old days if he had a pal in CR and not wholly impossible now.[1] The officer subsequently worked his way up to an honoured retirement. He was one of the most valued friends the thieves ever had. From the day when he managed to keep that record out, he was lost. Even now, in retirement, he has to co-operate.

The underworld will always push their luck. A bent copper is a gift from heaven in their eyes: but there is plenty of other useful material for the bending. We have already considered the case of the bellman. Today, sights set much higher, villains with financial ambitions do manage to influence 'respectable' people who would never have been in a position to encounter temptation in the old days. It is pleasant and flattering to most people to be offered a 'directorship' with fees (especially if there is a suggestion that these can be paid abroad and that the Inland Revenue are not going to hear about it) and many a man will shut his eyes to the morals of his fellow directors so long as the money comes in and he is 'not concerned with what they do'; nor, to be fair, is he always enlightened as to these details. But of course, he will not have been accosted unless he is useful so, when the crunch

[1] If they have gone over to microfilm, it is. A very important reform.

comes, he will find that he has to co-operate. Nor will he necessarily have gained much in the process. Thirty pieces of silver still does a lot: the price of dishonesty is unbelievably low at times.

Some of the people who got involved with gold-smuggling for 'kicks', often the owners of small sea-going aircraft, subsequently found that they had got to do it again when they did not want to or had to help with the disposal of stolen money through Swiss bank-accounts which they had been discovered to own. They get used as 'drops' too. Stolen property sometimes goes through the trembling hands of people of good character (officially) who have managed to get themselves into the power of people who know how to manipulate them. Boastful talk in Continental bars with slick new friends has been the undoing of many. Anything goes: if drug smuggling and peddling are not cracked down upon efficiently, corruption of this type can always present a menace, and the famous small packets[2] sealed in a particular way which must be unbroken on delivery, already pass through 'respectable' luggage, though this is only private enterprise and not organised on any scale. The seeds of creeping corruption are sown by the 'respectable' society itself and this is what is so disturbing. Now that it has become a matter of course to do down the income-tax man and to admire 'sharp' business, it hardly lies in our mouths to complain that the 'un-legitimate' world has exploited our loss of morality. There would, it is said, be no thieves without the fences: but there would be no fences unless there were thieves to support them. Similarly, corruption is a two-way process. There is nothing particularly new in the facts of corruption except for industrial espionage which is a relatively new aspect, but this does not concern the underworld as a general rule; what is noticeable is the scale on which it is practised. It was around in the eighteenth century; *The Beggar's Opera* commented upon it and its underlying motive – profit. Says Peachum, 'Money, wife, is the true fuller's earth for reputations: there is not a spot or stain but what it can take out. A rich rogue nowadays is fit company for any gentleman: and the world, my dear, hath not such a contempt for roguery as you imagine.' But

[2] Heroin – only paid for if not tampered with.

contacts between the two worlds were scarcer then. 'Gentlemen' today do consort much more with rogues: the fuller's earth of the bribe has made dishonesty exciting and called dishonesty fun. The eighteenth century was as material a period as today; indeed, most times are material in outlook when you get down to it, since man is greedy and selfish whether he admits it or disguises it under other names. Material prosperity today has done nothing to diminish crime at all social levels, and the facts underline the curious truth that poverty seems to have little connection with crime, stealing to live being a much smaller part of law-breaking than obtaining what you ought not to obtain in order to have a gay life on it.

The underworld tempter is well aware of what his bribes are doing, and frequently shows great contempt for his victim. Said one to me, 'Well, I never thought the day would come when I should get a gentleman like So-and-So on the hook. He ought to know better.' (I was not surprised, having observed unprofessional conduct on So-and-So's part before now.) But further comment was more difficult to deal with. 'If I had stuck to printing', he said, 'which was my legit. as a kid, I'd never have had the fun I've had.' (True, unfortunately.) 'But you know, since I've known John' (who is an accountant) 'he's opened my eyes to a lot of things that go on in business. I can't see the difference between what he does and what we do, except that he gets away with it and we often don't. He's had three grand out of my lot since the autumn – okay, he's worked for it, but what the hell does he think he's doing being big with me? He seems to think *he's* quite another cup of tea. Well, I know what my old dad would have said. "Len, my boy!", it would have been, "just you go ahead and take what you can off him. He's out of his class and he doesn't know the form. But don't you trust him further than you can see. He's a wrong 'un." But I don't know', said Len dolefully, 'There don't seem to be many about you can trust.' A pause. ' 'Course he's lost class all round, but I don't suppose he cares so long as the money keeps coming in. Things are queer today.'

One begins to get a tendency to moralise by association with these censorious underworld. There is something more distasteful about this brand of crookedness than the suborning of night-watchmen and such by people whose whole living is crime. Len's dad was right; they *ought* to know better. A modern phenomenon, it is on the increase; and it is, potentially a most serious fact of underworld life today. Press and politicians concentrate on denouncing Mafia, which seems to have taken the place of yellow perils, bolshie scares and nameless orgies as a good fill-in when hard news is scarce. It is American Cosa Nostra in most cases but Mafia is a more emotive word and sounds more sinister. Gambling and drugs are the subject matter of these stories and there is certainly grave danger in both possibilities. But what could in the long run be far worse than either is manipulation by crooks of any nationality, first of anything financial and then of political matters.

Such forebodings are not far-fetched as things are going today. Already we have seen in England reputable people conned into business enterprises with strange fellow-directors whose records were unkown to the innocent partners or, sometimes, unsearched for. To say that the subsequent discovery was frequently embarrassing to innocent parties is an understatement but, human nature being what it is, even the innocent tend to rationalise their actions and it takes a good deal to make a man of substance admit that he has been had for a sucker. He will almost invariably begin to say that his friends have been misjudged. This fact is well known to the underworld,[3] who have for ages taken advantage of the knowledge that the honest man, who gives honest alibi evidence about something that he has been induced to believe took place on the wrong day, will maintain to the Day of Judgement that his evidence is correct. It is, of course, the old saying that 'A man convinced against his will, is of the same opinion still.' One of the most sensible High Court Judges of our times once said in my hearing that the honest witness who had been persuaded of a wrong fact was the most dangerous ally of the criminal. The conned businessman will, in the majority of cases do anything he can to cover up – and believe himself to be in the right!

[3] And Counsel whose advice and warnings often fall on angry or unwilling ears!

Backwards and forwards from Britain to the United States fly faceless, well-heeled people, sometimes connected putatively with the buying of antiques, sometimes involved with the purchase of real property, all legal enough but with something in the background; shady, in that unmistakeable way which is not quite tangible but apparent. Such emissaries are always to be found in the West End (certain hotels know them better than others) and sooner or later they will be seen in the company of members of the underworld. Their business is, in many cases, the investment of Cosa Nostra money in profitable enterprises: Mafia money is as good as anybody else's and turns up all over the place. Since it is unwise for them to spend too much time in Britain, and their business takes them all over the world anyway, 'reliable' agents are employed, and this means two-way traffic, with the London underworld plying between this country and the States and making a lot of new friends in the process.

The underworld who get bitten with the American criminal's way of life do not often return to mere 'grafting' in the day-to-day sense. They have tasted bigger game. They come back stunned by the wealth and influence their American bosses seem to enjoy. 'Do you know, an American Air Force plane picked us up – just like that', said the awestruck grafter. 'You wouldn't believe it – he's only got to lift the phone and there's three senators jumping to his orders.' 'Bought a special apartment for me to use, in the city. 'Course, I stayed there. Cost eighty-five thousand quid, it did, with the gear in it, and as for food, well, he owns the best restaurant in the town and I just had to tell them what to send.' Useless to suggest to these enthusiasts that *they* are the conned. A thieves' paradise is being dangled before their eyes: they think that they are in on the big world at last and they are prepared to enslave themselves to their new masters. 'Made a wonderful impression, they tell me', said another satisfied cat's-paw. 'They think the world of me.' What a hope!

On these trips, sometimes individual, sometimes package deals to Las Vegas, that El Dorado of the gambler where everything, including the girls, is laid on; where anyone with the password can contact the barons of the American underworld scene, suitable siftings from the English underworld see and become accustomed to the American situation, where political graft is an accomplished and accepted fact, though it can be exaggerated and is. Nor is it difficult in democratic days, when an educated accent is no longer essential either for MP or businessman, for a plausible character to transplant his American experience into home soil and to work himself into suitable company, back in England. Here he can be used to establish the first bridgehead in his masters' interests, which will, of course, appear completely innocent of any sinister connections. Sooner or later, a lobby could be created in the interests of their employers. We are proud of our Parliament: we are proud of a virtually incorruptible Civil Service. 'It could not happen here' has been said and said again. But it could. The authorities were saying exactly the same thing about drugs. It was impossible for a journalist to sell information on the progress of drug-addiction as told me in the States a few years back, various editors considering that it was exaggerated and the authorities maintaining[4] (rather patronisingly, I thought) that everything was under control. In the event, five thousand words then written have been so accurately prophetic that even a journalist hardened by long experience of frustration could be forgiven for a spot of nail-biting. In our complex economy, where even the Common Market is beyond the comprehension of intelligent electors, there is ample opportunity for lobbies in disreputable interests to creep in before anyone can spot them. If this happens, it will be through the corruptibility or – worse perhaps – the folly of respectable men.[5]

The Reformation – and I speak as a Protestant – survived in England mainly because when Catholic estates were broken up and given to Protestants, it was a *sine qua non* of the bargain

[4] Not my invention. Contemporary official statements make sad reading now.

[5] At a dinner-party in Chester Square the same evening that I was writing this, corroboration of this sort of thing was supplied by one of our most respected legislators. He was relating his surprise over mysterious telephone calls from, first, Canada and then the Bahamas, suggesting that he could lend his name profitably to a board of directors. He is rather a tough proposition and countered by questions so searching that the caller rang off and has not yet reappeared. 'I'd heard of this sort of thing', he added, 'but I never thought it could happen to me!' Well, it *has* happened and to a lot of people who have not got X's good sense.

that he who held them remained Protestant. If that isn't a warning about the manipulation of respectable men, I don't know what is! Les (Catholic when in prison, on account of a more varied diet such as fish on Fridays and chapel outings which at least make a change) has just returned from the States on 'business', where, of all things, he has been with a high ecclesiastic who is reputedly head of a certain mob. I don't think I shall enlarge Les's knowledge of the Reformation!

Chapter 9

ARE CRIMINALS ALL TORIES?

Anyone who attempts to depict the underworld scene objectively lays himself open to the charge that he is 'siding with them', 'condoning crime', 'has lost his moral sense' and similar criticisms. But the accusation is unjust. One cannot mix moral judgements with objective reporting. It is no use calling the wolf a naughty dog : he may belong to the same species, but he is a totally different sort of dog from the fireside pet : only the naturalist who is prepared to observe the wolf in his own habitat, obeying or disobeying the pack laws, will be in a position to judge whether particular wolves are good or bad dogs of their own breed.

So with the criminal. In his private life, he is not a different species. Like Shylock, if you prick him, he will bleed, if you tickle, him, he will laugh. He is a human being who rejects our codes and accepts another. Actually, the analogy with domestic dog and wolf is fairly accurate. He is still the hunting animal that man used to be. Once within his cave, snug and warm with the loot won from his more domestic brother, underworld man is much like everyone else. National characteristics are as sharply defined there as elsewhere : cultures tend to lag a little behind, underworld social habits being, as a rule, a few years behind latest trends. Underworld characters have duly observed the manners and customs of polite society but take a bit of time to find their way about them. No one likes to make a fool of himself in unknown territory and basic insecurity in the underworld is very prevalent. Socially, they are no Columbuses.

So the English criminal of the present day is snobbish; keeps women in their place; has, on the whole, old-fashioned double moral standards about sex; does not use nearly such bad language in front of 'ladies' as he hears elsewhere; is a good husband as a rule (but not to the extent of keeping out of trouble); is almost always a devoted father (with the same proviso); is rarely anything but kind to children and animals; is mildly jingoistic, and thinks highly of the Queen, if not of her hospitality. He also has a high regard for British justice but never regards it as being done. He grumbles, like his respectable counterpart, about a lot of things and, like him, very seldom does more about them than talk. He is very keen on his rights and has no conception at all of corresponding duties. He likes his food, his drink and a happy home.

As I have said elsewhere, any member of this community is automatically part of a resistance movement against law and order. So the private life of the underworld is more agitated than that of the law-abiding citizen, who does not start at every unexpected caller's knock and does not feel bound to peep through net curtains if a car[1] pulls up outside without any reason that he can think of. If anything so disorganised as the average criminal's life can be said to be organised, a good deal of planning does seem to go on to deal with frequent interruptions. Not many of them emulate a client of my husband's, a conscientious objector during the war, who filled in his form 'Means of support' with the frank and hopeful answer, 'God will provide : wife working'; but those who go to prison at fairly regular intervals are glad to have a wife who can be reasonably independent and there are a number of businesses, such as small shops, which get more attention in misfortune than in prosperity. It is also always convenient to have property in the wife's name. Legal aid, the best thing that ever happened from their point of view, gets exploited in this way as well as others, though prestige sometimes demands the privately-paid defence. A good deal of underworld time also, by my reckoning, appears to be taken up with mysterious telephone calls raising the wind for some pal in trouble.

For they do stand together, though it is doubtful whether this is due to true friendship or to custom. Few calls for help fall to the ground. A man who goes to prison can almost always find the pal who will look after his family. Money is lent, paid back,

[1] Few underworld homes neglect simple precautions, such as an 'eye' in the front door. But some go much further; Asking for the 'ladies' when visiting one home, I found that retreat, just outside the back door, complete with the store of potatoes – and a rope ladder, which hooked neatly over the garden wall, providing an escape-route to a side-road.

welshed, forgiven or pursued all the time.[2] Nearly always, all gets forgiven in the end and the same defaulter will be able to raise the next loan. It is the world of easy come, easy go. I sometimes envy the ease with which friendship is exploited. Fleet Street is not so charitable!

Occasionally, things go wrong, even among friends. A long guerrilla skirmish went on amongst one small group who mixed ordinary screwing with all sorts of con-tricks (said one of them of another, 'He couldn't add up the laundry book straight') and who, sharing a flat, a procedure which was unbelievable to most of their acquaintances, kept up internecine squabbles reminiscent of some married couples.

Eventually, there was a real barney: A accused B – with truth – of having done him of five 'grand'. It was, I think, connected with a truth-is-stranger-than-fiction episode of having rented a castle especially to strip an entire lead roof from it; but I may be wrong about this, in which case I apologise to the injured party. B, realising that things were too hot for him, 'went missing', as the saying goes and remained missing for a considerable period. News then reached A that B was around again, under another name and with a considerable bank-balance. Raising three allies, he broke into B's new flat to await his return, pounced upon him, floored him and sat on his prostrate body, explaining in simple language that death was imminent if the five grand was not instantly forthcoming.

By repute, B would rather lose his life than five grand. But he feared the manner of despatch. 'Are you going to shoot me?' he inquired. 'No!' came the answer. 'Is it a coshing?' he said, rather shakily. After all, shooting is relatively painless. 'No!' came an even grimmer reply, whilst his head was banged on the floor by way of showing earnest. 'Not the knife, boy, is it?', whimpered the victim, in a tone of voice which would have cheered all those who believe in the deterrent value of cold steel. '*Yes*' roared the chorus in the back row, now swollen to five.

He capitulated. 'Five grand *now*,' said the chorus. The bank was closed for the afternoon, but A knew that B's substantial

[2] As I write, a wife has just rung me to say that £200 has been 'lent' for a defence in a matter of two hours.

balance ensured courteous attention from his bank-manager. So 'Get on the blower, boy, and get it fixed', said A.

This done, a procession set off to the bank. It then occurred to A that it would be as well for them not to sit in a large car outside the bank, as B might doublecross and suggest to the manager that a raid was imminent. So the most city-like member of the gang, now grown to six, agreed to go with the respected customer 'just friendly', whilst the car waited round the corner. But B is a very old hand. With the money in his briefcase, he asked the manager for the 'gents'; and made his exit at the back. Meanwhile, his escort dare not follow but, coming out, spotted B running down a side-street and started in pursuit.

B, now running fast, thought even faster. He rushed into a block of high-class flats, shouting to the porter, 'Help, help! There are robbers after me! Call the police!' The escort melted into the background, the waiting car vanished quicker than thought; and so did B; for when the porter raised his head from the 999 call, there was no one there. He must have thought that his lunchtime beer had had something very wrong with it!

The sequel? All pals together not long after. The five grand was settled for at three-and-a-half and successful skullduggery has flourished several times since then. Which illustrates the point that it is wonderful how they cling together.

Class distinction in the underworld is as real and as firm as the old caste system of India. There is a general grading (professional) into 'well-respected' and the rest, the rest including classes which are called by many names, some being as scornful as 'dirt' and occasionally 'animals'. Socially, skilful jewel thieves rank highest, their wives not condescending to much geniality with those of lesser rank. 'Who does she think she is!' has been said by more than one indignant wife when the wife of a lower-class accomplice has ventured social contacts. Violence used to put people down many a grade, as 'unprofessional', which indeed it was: today, it is so much part of the picture that, provided skill and success attend its doers, few except the old think too badly of it. Upper-class ranking also sticks to bellmen, 'petermen' and specialists in skilled jobs such as banks. Trying to see whether skill or success means the most, one comes to the conclusion that they are really the same thing. The skilful does tend to make more money and he is also probably blessed with more social graces. The con-man is in a variable category, but sometimes he is 'well-respected'. It depends on his clientele. If he confines his attentions to legitimate prey, he can be popular; and also much admired, particularly if he is good for a laugh: the woes of others are a jolly topic around the clubs. But if he preys on his own kind – and a number do – and if, as often happens, he does a bit of informing on the side, he is hated, feared, and kept in a mild sort of Coventry. The same applies to the 'fixer', i.e. the man who acts as go-between police and criminal and is frequently used as the briber. Off-hand, as a matter of fact, I can only think of one who is really liked and invited to dinner. Most of them are regarded as useful 'dirt'! One, at least, is an 'animal'.

Most of these lower caste underworld are only visible in the pubs and spielers of their own neighbourhood where they hang around hoping to be hired, as this is more profitable than individual 'work'. Otherwise, they are mainly to be seen in prison yards. With the exception of some 'sharp', small-time villains, they form that fraction of the underworld which looks what it is – moronic, brutal and definitely not part of anyone's social scene. Their 'betters' know them all right: they use them too; but they do not ask them to dinner. One deserves attention as something out of the ordinary.

This particular man with a record as long as his arm gave me a lot of information about a protection racket, he being at war with its executives, for which reason he cannot be identified, though he is not sharp enough to mind this. He is not without a nice sense of humour, carrying 'Contractor to HM Government' on his letter-heading, a joke which, on inquiry, turned out to be that he had done so much time in both His and Her Majesty's Service, sewing mailbags and such, that he considered he had a right to record the fact. Our first meeting was a little strained. As I approached his office, with the friend who was introducing me, we saw a gun being poked through the letter-box. The friend took to his heels but I walked on, reckoning that the amateur marksman was unlikely to shoot a woman: which proved to be the case. He had merely taken precautions against being rushed by the enemy. As he had had to deal with a petrol bomb a few days earlier, this was understandable if alarming, though the possession of a gun is not quite the legal thing – he is certainly low on the list of those who can be trusted with one.[3]

I mention him for two reasons. He is so 'reliable' (i.e. will carry out anything he undertakes – an awesome thought) that he is 'well-respected' enough to have broken through the class barrier and to be admitted to some meeting-places from which his equals are excluded. He is also, though violent, far from bright and, I imagine, the terror of any nick to which he is consigned, a most faithful and considerate husband to a slowly dying wife, having kept out of trouble on his own telling for this reason only. Honour to whom honour is due.

[3] He showed me the gun with some pride. I am no expert but am told, on describing it to one, that it would blow a hole the size of a large orange in the victim. My friend was quite the gentleman: he wiped my fingerprints off with the greatest care, saying, 'You never know what they'll fix on you.'

Chapter 10

THE UNDERWORLD IN TROUBLE

When Dickens drew the portrait of the Artful Dodger he depicted for all time an accurate picture of underworld intelligence. Few of its citizens may be top-heavy with learning but few indeed are deficient in that instinct for survival with which goes artfulness and a sort of basic craftiness. Unfortunately for them, they are also lacking in foresight, which is why so many get themselves ever deeper into trouble when arrested. Faced with emergency, the unhappy crook usually has the bright idea that he can invent a story which will get him out of the immediate trouble; so he pours out the first fairy-tale that comes into his head. It all sounds splendid until, in the cold light of day, it becomes apparent that none of it can possibly be substantiated, his luckless Counsel frequently having to put up this hopeless story. Many a barrister's heart has been wounded by the ingratitude of a client who has supplied him with the faulty story and has then blamed him for its failure on presentation. On the other hand Counsel who has known when to shut up, with resultant acquittal, is often despised for his success. 'Didn't make any fight at all', complains the client to his friends over an acquittal pint. 'Now X – there *is* a fighter for you. He knew how to tell the Judge where he got off!' X's continuous war with the Judge, together with what the gallery consider to be real fighting tactics in cross-examination, have in fact resulted in bringing out the one answer which finished *his* client with the jury and ended in three years for him. But X's performance has been admired and he will quite probably get a repeat performance. The same ill-deserved applause goes to the smaller number of dishonest solicitors who somehow manage to keep up the myth that they can 'fix' the police.[1] Perhaps they do –

[1] They are incredible people, these conning solicitors, and it is difficult to make the underworld believe your evidence. I once had a hilarious interview

sometimes – but if they ever do contrive a successful bribe, any crook ought to know by now that they keep a handsome portion of the money paid over, judging by the amounts said to be paid and allowing for the customary underworld exaggeration. It is one of the most frustrating situations that arise in underworld contacts when one is so often asked for help, gives it first in the form of advice to go to a completely straight firm, has one's advice ignored, and then is appealed to again, too late. The Courts know the black sheep and consequent prejudice is natural enough; again something which you cannot beat into underworld heads. I have often heard Bench, off-duty, smiling sadly, say 'Well, one knew the sort of client X's firm take on.' The disappearance of another (this time only a managing clerk) also elicited the remark, 'There has been a great deterioration in the quality of the alibis at such and such a court.'

Dodging, twisting and turning, the thief in trouble makes things more and more difficult for himself. I am not exaggerating when I say that I have never – absolutely never – when in possession of the facts, known a story put up in Court by a professional crook that was one hundred per cent true. It may not have been meant to deceive in principle; rather that, even with good and sound evidence on his side, it seems impossible for the man in trouble not to attempt to gild the lily and pile up what he thinks will help. Sometimes I think it is almost a sporting throw by people who cannot resist a bet. One of the bright ideas is always the alibi, phoney if a genuine one is not available. Such was a recent case in which a serious miscarriage of justice has probably been done. Straightforward conduct might well have saved the day. The case must not be identified, since the man is rather well known, but roughly speaking, the facts are as follows.

with one, who broke off our discourse to conduct a telephone conversation with, it appeared, a member of the Cabinet, laced with such remarks as 'That's very good of you, sir. I appreciate it. We only did our best. Certainly, sir – I'll speak to the Home Secretary tomorrow.' Unfortunately for him, my secretary was watching in the outer office. She slipped a note into my hand before the end of the conversation, so that I was able to say to him, as he rang off and began to tell me of a forensic triumph, 'What a splendid performance, Mr Y! Was it a tape or just impromptu gagging? You have your secretary's timing very nicely rehearsed.' Not the only one apparently. Lord Northcliffe had the same little habit, it is said!

Only too familiar a figure in the prisons, B had recently come out after a long sentence. He was arrested, behaving quite quietly (which is unusual for him!) and charged with a robbery which he probably did not commit, for rather obvious reasons which cannot be given here, though I consider it likely that he handled the proceeds at some stage. However, he was not charged with this. There was then some trouble over alleged police demands for money; at the point where everything was lined up to trap these officers if the story was true,[2] the demands ceased. Meanwhile, despite continued warnings, a dubious solicitor ('They say he is in with the CID, so B wants him') had been engaged: the brief was ill-prepared, Counsel not well instructed, the threatened police 'verballing'[3] took place. B was certainly at a disadvantage, to put it mildly. But what really sank him was the well-meant phoney alibi of a friend, who tried hard to help with what he thought would do. Unhappily, the exposure of the alibi – always a difficult matter to sustain, even when true – threw such discredit on the whole matter that B went down – and for a long, long time. It is sometimes *very* hard not to say, 'I told you so!'

As may be imagined, the two worlds in which I live make life difficult. Fortunately, coming of a legal family and imbibing legal etiquette with mother's milk, so to speak, I am able to survive the schizophrenic existence to which underworld acquaintanceships consign me. To do this circle justice, they do appear to know that 'certain people' (to which band my husband belongs) are not in the bribing stakes and are not going to be parties to the dodging and ducking that goes on. This does not prevent them from pouring it all out and having the occasional hopeful bash. It is all too apparent that they consider women to be of baser clay. There is, I think, a faint hope that perhaps

[2] Since this sort of allegation is often made, I will add that, after listening in to a certain telephone conversation, I was sufficiently convinced of impropriety to take steps as indicated.

[3] There may be some readers who do not know this term, which means, in our vernacular, the giving by the police of either wholly or partially untruthful evidence of what a person said or is alleged to have said. It is most bitterly resented in the underworld and is very common. I can speak from experience, though not in court, having had to do something fairly brisk about a young constable who tried it on over a parking offence. He did not realise that he had caught tartars!

something might be put over in marital confidence. 'You can tell him the law has been fixed', says one. 'Nothing to worry about with that inspector.' 'I want to explain it all to *you*', says another. 'Of course, I shan't say this to my brief.' There follows a yarn of such complexity that I am completely baffled, coming to the surface at intervals with what I hope is the correct comment but often aware that my reply is not what it ought to be. 'I *told* you about Majorca', says my confidant angrily. 'Don't you take nothing in?' Names float past me until suddenly I clutch at the straw of a familiar incident and come to just as the remark is made, 'Course, if you were to tell your husband this, it might help. Not that he's to put the story up, but it would help for him to know what's what.' 'No', I say, 'I'm afraid it wouldn't. He gets his instructions from his brief, and', I add, 'if you were to tell him what you've told me, he wouldn't appear for you. You know that as well as I do.' 'Well, just tell him it's all right with the law. All fixed.' The sequel, naturally, is that I say nothing: it is *not* all right with the law, which goes into the witness-box and perfectly properly gives the correct evidence; and the next two happenings are to be rung up in the small hours by the sorrowing family and the addition of another visiting day to my list, plus more harrowing correspondence from HM's prisons.

Life would be much simpler if at any stage the underworld, going crook or going straight, learned the economic value of *truth*. This extends to boasting, and both wishes are virtually impossible ones. Being 'big' is another underworld characteristic, a very understandable one too, which one cannot but sympathise with – and deplore. A wife once said desparingly, 'He always has to be the big one. It's always getting him into trouble.' She might have added that vast sums of money 'lent' to friends to show his size, had to be recovered by burglary! With a chip on the shoulder, the outlaw with wolf's head finds it sweet consolation to boast of his prowess, his loot, his friendships with notorious villains (if he is staying crooked), his high-class acquaintances (if he is trying to go straight). It often backfires. One tragic case meant the end of a genuine business, worked up for ten years, all with a conviction trumped up on entirely false evidence[4] but where untrue boasting about the capital A had acquired gave substance to the suggestion that he had been involved in a gangster activity. Being 'big' runs right through this society, sometimes ludicrously, sometimes pathetically.

[4] Not the police, This was a deliberate and spiteful revenge for a fancied insult by another of the fraternity, my non-favourite con-man, as a matter of fact.

Chapter 11

OF MURDER AND MAYHEM

We have our discussions in the Badger's and we have our philosophers too. We do not go along with Greeks of old in considering all topics suitable for discussion. Some, such as the whereabouts of absent friends or indelicate inquiries as to shareouts, are described as 'highly personal' and are dealt with by freezing out the inquirer. But there is no objection to the general probing of manners and customs and, if self-criticism is rare, that of others is extremely common.

So I tried to find out, one sultry evening, just what was thought about the ethics of theft. It was a peaceful evening. Nothing much had been happening in the world, no big jobs had been going around for a few weeks (the underworld was human after all; and heatwaves and extreme cold make work unwelcome there as in the respectable world); the gods of racing seemed to have favoured the wrongdoer for some days and the most likely candidate for 'turning-over' had fled to the States, a fact which, as all knew, was also well known to the Law. So there was less chance of a sudden turning-over. 'Lucky for him he's got rich relations there.' The rich relations, as far as could be gathered, (another avenue not to be pursued) had connections with Cosa Nostra, though only respectable ones, that is to say, connected with the investment of Mafia money; you might say, business not 'business': anyway, the fugitive was causing no trouble to his fellow members.

I did not dare to mention John Gay, thought to be an unpleasant eccentricity of mine ('*beggars* indeed!') but had come freshly from one of the many revivals and had Mat o' the Mint's words still in my mind: 'We retrench the superfluities of mankind. The world is avaricious and I hate avarice. A covetous fellow, like a jackdaw, steals what he was never meant to enjoy, for the sake of hiding it. These are the robbers of mankind; for money was made for the free-hearted and generous and where is the injury of taking from another what he hath not the heart to enjoy?' It was interesting to ponder on whether the modern thief still justified his depredations in the same way. An opportunity came when tribute was paid to one of the youngsters, who had shown what was considered to be proper feeling in a matter of a divorce.

This boy had married a young girl who had had a jackdaw's eye for jewellery. One particular piece she had coveted was a highly identifiable clip, which was, I think, in her birth-stone and had been spotted by her at a Command Performance some time previously. 'Never left him alone she didn't till he nicked it', said Alf, shaking his head. 'Kept on at him proper till he got it set up for her birthday present. And it didn't bring her luck, 'cos look at them now.' To cut a long story short, there had been a pretty up-and-down whilst the husband served a short, sharp sentence for something else and the net result had been a broken marriage and the flight of the wife plus clip to a more respectable home with a more respectable husband. Not the sort of story to commend itself to the club. What had impressed them was the conduct of the late husband, who, with unbelieveable folly (in my eyes) and generosity (in theirs) had allowed her to keep this bit of 'hot' jewellery 'because she was fond of it!' A perfect example of sentimentality which should never be confused with sentiment. There were favourable comments on this, though others rightly thought he was taking a chance. 'But didn't it occur to any of you', I said finally, 'that the real owner might have been fond of it too? Does it ever occur to you that people like the things you nick and are unhappy when they are stolen?' After the inevitable silence, it became clear that these rude words demonstrated that I simply did not understand. 'They' don't miss things, I was told. 'They' get insurance and that's okay. 'They' can always get something else – look how 'they' dodge income-tax. Why anyone could tell me the sacks of 'cabbage' that 'they' keep hidden in the house because 'they' get paid in cash and keep it from the income-tax man. 'They', in brief, have property but no feelings; and this is another underworld belief which can't be broken through.

I was once trying to impress upon an old burglar that the path to recidivism was not the only road to follow after early dishonesty. I explained the story told in the Preface that during one short period I had stolen pennies and once a sixpence from my mother, who never allowed me any pocket-money as a child; and had hidden the booty under the stair-carpet (carefully spaced out). Curiously enough, he too had concealed his early thefts in exactly the same place and, this happy unity of conduct and ritual being established, I thought it was a good moment to drive home the point that a temporary lapse of this sort need not result in life-long crime. I thought this had impressed itself upon him: I was quite wrong. Three weeks later, I was introduced by him to a new contact with the words 'This is Peta Fordham. You can trust her a million per cent. One of us. Used to nick when she was young: gave up when she married W.G.F.' My husband nearly died of laughing when he heard this version of my life-story. I shall never live it down (or is it up?) in the underworld, and it never will be forgotten. It throws light on some of the difficulties facing those who go about hoping to reform people!

But things are very different if underworld themselves are robbed. Let an *au pair*[1] girl help herself to some small piece of property and there are screams of protest. The heisting of thieves' own cars is a source of real indignation: whilst, as everybody knows, to steal loot from a fellow-thief or to do down someone over the proceeds thereof, is the ultimate sin, leading to violence and, on occasion, to murder.

Underworld attitudes to killing have deteriorated in the last few years. In the words of one old acquaintance 'Crime was definitely more high-class then. Definitely.' This odd statement may or may not be accurate; but what he was driving at was something to which one can assent. Nothing of recent years has illustrated this so clearly as the reaction to the gruesome kidnapping of Mrs Muriel McKay,[2] the wife of one of the best-known newspapermen in London.

[1] No underworld family ever seems to lack domestic assistance. Perhaps it is higher wages: whatever the cause, beautiful *au pairs* are always at hand for underworld babies.

[2] See page 94, footnote 4.

I was away in France when the news of Mrs McKay's abduction broke. Twenty-four hours later, the London underworld was humming with theories and rumours, united at this stage in admiration of what appeared to be a master stroke. 'Good' crime, by which is meant in these circles, profitable, well-organised activities, had been scarce (for a number of reasons) though violent, snatch-type jobs had been on the increase. So anything involving a putative sum of a million pounds had professional appeal. The subsequent proceedings had also been followed with close attention : the macabre is popular reading.

What was puzzling to all was that no one knew who was responsible. There was the usual turnover of every possible miscreant by the police, to the fury of those with something else to hide. One by one, by both 'the Law' and the fraternity, the regulars were checked off. Feverish curiosity seized the underworld and, since nobody could be shopped, talk was quite open in any company – which is rare indeed. The immediate assumption was that it was an Australian gang, a theory no doubt fed by the fact that both the Murdochs and the McKays had so many links there. The shoplifting gangs, who are 'well-respected' in the London underworld for sheer audacity and professional competence, had been boasting that their exodus to the Continent was *réculer pour mieux sauter* and that big things were on the way. The robbery at the Hotel Crillon had been credited to them and this kidnapping sounded to underworld ears like a Ned Kelly follow-up. 'It's them all right – scooped us again' were the opening, melancholy words of my first telephone-call, one of a flood which, for the first time in my experience, actually sought information *from* the press.

Charlie, aged twenty-three, raises his eyes from the racing page and has plenty to say. He has been in trouble all his life and has had contacts with most of the protection rackets. He has also done a lot of small shabby crimes.

Charlie has attended as much of the McKay trial as he could (or says he has) and his only real criticism of the whole business is of the amateur methods. 'Grabbing the wrong bird is one thing', he says, 'well, even if they had, well, look, keeping her hanging around – it's not clever. Bloody amateurs. They want to get a few good men on it and where's your trouble?' Charlie's friend chimes in, 'No point in feeding her to the pigs.[3] She's worth more alive than dead, and any silly bastard ought to know that.' A con-man says that he is drinking and doesn't want that sort of talk here but the young contingent, pressed, admit that they couldn't care less whether one woman more or less gets killed on a job. 'Well, we've all got to die, haven't we?' Criticism of this particular kidnapping is economic and a singularly nasty story emerges as to the fate of some Pakistanis who, alleges one youth, were suffocated in the fumes of the boat-engine when their smuggler discovered they had done him over the money. One older man who has done a recent stretch in a Continental gaol says that good money is hard to come by and that he discussed kidnapping as an income-booster with a Belgian robber. I have a sudden fear that this may be putting ideas into the heads of the Charlie section: most of the elders say that they would not work with A, on *that* job, while one fifty-year-old semi-retired burglar says 'Kidnapping is very un-British.' Nobody thinks this is funny.

I raised the McKay case a week later with an intelligent contact. In his words 'it sorted the men from the boys', whatever that meant. He did not reveal his own feelings, but took me on a tour of three pubs and two spielers, where we chatted for short periods. Few men under thirty cared what had happened. 'Her old man should have paid up and not tried to be clever,' said one, perhaps the most callous. Several thought it extremely funny that a 'nosy pair' of respectable people had wrecked the Yard's second ransom trap by telling the local police of a dumped suitcase; they 'had to do her after that' said another. 'Wouldn't you?' 'Chicken' said his friend. 'I wouldn't let one grand slip like that, let alone the lot.' The older group were as shocked, on the whole, as most of us are, though without compassion. Violence came through even there. 'Never mind about trying them. Put the buggers, excuse me lady! up against a wall and shoot them.' Twenty years ago, much more horror would have been expressed and, in fact, the most understanding comment I heard came from a murderer,

[3] **A horrible theory, discredited at the trial.**

well-known, and recently freed, now nearing sixty.[4] Violence has become a short cut, as opposed to carefully planned and skilled craftsmanship, as to which, 'It costs,' said one. 'Look what the bellmen charge.'

[4] In prison again – as usual! But not for murder this time.

Chapter 12

GANGSTERS IN GANGLAND

Nothing shows the primitive character of the underworld more clearly than its inhabitants' attitude to death. Natural death is unmentionable – a thing to be warded off with a charm, nothing to do with the living, an accident which happens to other people. Deaths which happen as the result of violence, whether that of crook or victim, are quite different and are merely something in the way of business, as are the lesser results of violence. In much the same way, the eighteenth-century Mat o' the Mint lightly dismissed the presence of his brother's hanged corpse 'among the otamies in Surgeons' Hall'.

A certain split attitude applies both to criminals and to their victims. There was much discussion at the time about the torture and deaths arising out of the Richardson and Kray cases. The ordinary underworld was very frightened indeed of these two gangs. Stories used to go round of cement coffins and bodies dumped in wells and some normally tough members of the fraternity took great care to keep out of the way of either mob. The situation was a bit complicated, however, by the fact that both gangs had been used, before they became dominant, for carrying out revenge work that the more finicky underworld did not wish to do themselves. There is no suggestion, by the way, that gangster leaders themselves went around 'cutting' – i.e. knifing, or shooting victims for other people's benefit. What happened was that they had for a long time been collecting followers, often of low-grade mentality, who would do any job for a fee: such leaders were consequently useful to contact and could 'arrange' things on profitable terms. Grander members of the underworld used to say in those days that they would not recognise what they then called 'riff-raff' or ruder names, should they find themselves in the same West End haunt. They had to drop this behaviour as the gangsters rose in the world and were then prone to be very polite indeed – especially in the West End.

To understand the way in which the Richardson and Kray gangs obtained their power for a comparatively short time in the underworld, it is illuminating to follow their history in brief. The complexities of their various villainies have filled several books to overflowing and all that we need consider here is the general picture of a phenomenon which happened once and will, in all probability, not happen again, for a long time at least.

Both gangs, led in each case by a pair of brothers, the Krays being identical twins, rose from obscure beginnings in areas noted for the production of trouble. The Richardsons came from Camberwell: the Krays from the heart of the East End. The Richardsons began as scrap-dealers with a mixture of genuine and dishonest business: the Krays, good as young boxers but tearaways from the start, had a short time as professional boxers, a phase interrupted by National Service. Some have said that, had they been left alone without this break, they would have made the grade in the sporting world. This is not very likely. From the earliest moment, even those members of the underworld who admire pluck and excuse most things in a game fighter, reported something sinister about Kray methods. 'They'll be killers one day', said a quiet old rogue who made his living around the boxing and racing haunts. 'That Ronnie is a saddler.' It took me some time before realising that he meant 'sadist'. Early scraps with schoolmates had had sadistic violence in them and there had always been ugly tales.

The two gangs developed quite differently. The Richardsons, later to be associated with the Torture Case, were primarily interested in becoming financiers, an ambition not realised at first by their acquaintances to whom they appeared to be making the grade in fairly petty crime of the usual or unusual sort. The scrap-metal business was quickly supplemented by a series of premises from which were sold cheap sundries, often stolen or, on occasion, long-firm frauds were successfully carried out. From this beginning they went on to create a protection racket in one-armed bandits in association with Frankie Fraser, known as

'Mad Frankie', a violent psychopathic criminal who has always been the terror of any nick which holds him and has, to quote one pal, 'been passed on like a hot potato by any Governor who can'. Frankie, extraordinarily popular with many respectable underworld because he is reputedly fearless (not surprisingly, considering his mental history), was reported to be going straight with a wholesale business in the one-armed bandits until he tied up with Eddie Richardson. Whether or not this was true, it was not long before a sizeable racket was established by the two of them over club-owners in the West End and elsewhere. It is, however, worth noting that respectable club-owners, as usual, had nothing to fear, contrary to what people often assume. Protection, which is another name for blackmail, only operates when there is a blackmailing hold to cling on to. The man who is carrying on a properly run club, at proper hours and without girls (or boys) in the background, can go to the police and seek real protection. It is the man who is trying to make quick, illegal profits who cannot. Old Alf, in the Badger's, always up in legal jargon, explained it very neatly. 'You might say it's contributory negligence.' The Richardsons[1] incidentally were not the only gang operating at this date. Rows over 'manors' were common, as they always are. Police behaviour was not reputedly impeccable at this time in Soho, and altogether it was a most unhappy period for the forces of law and order.[2]

From the profits of a lot of extremely successful and varied villainy, the Richardson brothers, to cut a long and complicated story short, began to see themselves in real money. There followed (everyday petty crime still being pursued, but mostly at a discreet distance, through hired men) the huge South African operation which was to result in battle, murder and sudden death all round, and which was, through the revenges taken with those

[1] Whatever view is taken of Eddie Richardson in the outside world, it is well known that he is an *extremely* popular fellow-prisoner in top-security. It makes one wonder!

[2] I don't know which of many gangs was responsible, but on one occasion in this district a girl was selected quite wantonly and thrown from a first-floor window, when protection money was not forthcoming. She recovered, but dared not inform.

who were considered disloyal, to lead Eddie and Charlie Richardson to exemplary sentences of imprisonment for life.

Our *Sunday Times*[3] team were in a position to follow this financial operation from an early date, thanks to tip-offs from scandalised underworld who 'shopped' the brothers in an almost unprecedented way, on account of torture reports that had already begun to leak out. We were all fairly unshockable; one does not deal in this kind of information and remain, like the late Mr Justice Vaisey, liable to raise outraged hands (literally) at the mention of corruption; but even hardened reporters were surprised, to put it mildly, by the respectability of the names that the brothers had managed to 'con' into assistance. Most of them, fortunately for public decency, found out in time: one at least ought to remain a faithful subscriber to the paper for the rest of his life and one or two more, when they found out that journalists were interested in perlite[4] deals, made rather more careful inquiries and got out.

The truth, I think, is that the brothers were on to a good thing and, if the business had been conducted ethically and efficiently, it might well have been a successful coup. What actually and predictably happened was that everyone in it immediately began to cheat the others: every so-called 'director' who remained when the respectable had quit schemed to run a racket himself! Reprisals began from an early stage and by now it is impossible to do more than surmise that the idea, in embryo, was a good one.

Police investigations began early on and this, though dilatory, was known to the brothers and their associates, and accelerated the process of getting rich quick – always disastrous. Anyway, to cut a very long story short and to miss out a host of sordid details that can be found elsewhere, a series of gang fights and killings, some internal clean-ups in the police and a lot of squealing from

[3] A hard life, the journalist's. We did not publish all we knew, on account of libel. Subsequently some of our best information was scooped. But the police owe us some gratitude.

[4] Perlite was the material involved in the biggest deal – a valuable building material, not widely distributed and originally and mainly found in Hungary, I believe.

a now thoroughly horrified underworld resulted in the end of Richardson activities for a considerable time.

In fairness to the brothers however and before considering the Kray gang, two points should be made. Torture – ingenious, disgusting and cruel – was meted out only to those who had offended against underworld codes, as part of the outfit. This fact may make little difference to us but it affects the underworld's view deeply. All sorts of rumours went around about the 'torture cellar' and those who had relatives near to the gang were terrified. But underworld condemnation was never so severe as it was for the Krays. 'They only done those who done them' was said over and over again – from a distance. (If you were nearer the view was apt to be different.) Snobbism, 'Disgusting – come from nothing', was a much more general condemnation from afar than pity for the victims or disapproval of cruelty.

The Krays were another kettle of fish altogether. Lust for power was what made them tick; and power involves money. Also there is a recurrent element of mental derangement of the most brutal and sadistic kind running through their story. Put objectively, it would be true to say that the Richardsons killed and tortured mainly in the way of business, the Krays (Ronnie, anyway) for pleasure as well. This view was expressed not so long ago by a youngster who had been a hanger-on of the gang, until literally shocked out of it into a return to petty thieving. He summarised the position thus: 'The Xs' (still active, though reduced in power and not nameable) 'kill for money, the Richardsons did it for business and the Krays for fun.' This sums up the viewpoint of a good many of his friends and contemporaries.

The Krays, as already said, began in the sporting world but were early on aware of the pickings to be had there, and they picked. Never averse to violence, they were talent-spotted (no pun intended) by Jack Spot – real name Comer – as 'minders' for some of his smaller protection rackets. They remained patrons of sport and, despite all the villainies that they were known to commit and all the horror that they eventually inspired in all right-minded crooks, there were those who, until the end, retained a sort of Robin Hood image of them. The reason was that although they were social climbers of the most persistent kind, continually photographed with such socialites or 'well-known personalities' as were mug enough to fall for the brothers' plausibility, they remained East Enders, never pretending to be anything else. They also subscribed large sums to charity. Most of these were just 'front' – a super-show-off to their important friends. But the East End was genuinely never forgotten. You have to dig deep indeed to find the one speck of decency in the careers of this pair. This loyalty to roots may have been it. There are still a few old dears in the East End who call Heaven's blessing on them. No one else is likely to.

No underworld character that I know considers Ronnie Kray as anything but mad and this is probably as accurate a view as that of any psychiatrist. Some of these had the same opinion and he did spend time in Long Grove, near Epsom, a mental hospital with which I have had dealings and which, until recently was the most sinister place of its kind that I have ever met. I am not nervous, but the long laurel-encrusted walks up to the wards were so macabre that I refused to visit there on my own after dark – and I have walked alone through raving Swedes in a locked compound without losing my cool! The thought of Ronnie Kray and the Long Grove of that date in conjunction is spine-chilling. Anyway, he got out of there by the simple device of exchanging identities temporarily with his twin and walking out to remain free for the statutory period.

Madness takes many forms and so little is known of it that even the lay may venture to have views on it. So far as it occurs in the underworld, madness and badness are closely connected. The late Father Martindale one remarked that he had never known a case of mental derangement developing in a man which brought out characteristics which were not already there; and I have often pondered on this. Father Martindale was not unacquainted with those who believed themselves to be Christ: Ronnie Kray's delusion was that he was a reincarnation of Al Capone, whose appearance and clothes he copied faithfully. A woman who was closer to the twins than most (Ronnie's homosexuality is common knowledge and girlfriends were not many) told me with revulsion of a conversation, before the horror of the

McVitie murder,[5] in which Ronnie spoke with excitement 'All twitching, he was', of his pleasure in seeing a slashed face 'burst open, like a flower, a lovely red flower, but it's better with a shooter'.

I used to watch the Krays, one of whose close companions I knew well, doing the big bully-boy act in the clubs. They really did live up to the image of the big gangster who simply forces his way through and, whatever they lacked, it was not character. Some poor little florist, for instance, would see his best roses picked up without payment and carried away. What they wanted, they took, and such was their hypnotic power, stemming from an unbelieveable confidence in themselves, that nobody took them on in time. As the money clocked up from every variety of racket, success became assured, in their world. There was plenty of employment for out-of-work hoodlums as Kray strong-arm men, 'rent-collectors'[6] and a myriad of small violent jobs. In the absence of a powerful top-gang to keep matters in check, there were really few other outlets for a rising (and often risen) generation in crime.

The 'Firm', as the gang was later known, had so many activities that we might as well skip most of the uninteresting ones, remarking in passing that one profitable and early one which became a hardy perennial and a great source of discord among members of the gang (who were as mutually distrustful as it is possible to be) was a levy on successful crimes, particularly the hi-jacking of lorries. As the associates of the gang grew – there are always little jackals around any such mob – the Krays were able to get tip-offs,[7] sometimes rewarded and sometimes not – of jobs in prospect. The blackmail was then on and the underworld were surprisingly flabby in their co-operation. This is the

[5] I am not normally one for suppression but the details of this crime are quite unsuitable for reading by the general public: a witness to it, used to gang violence, said that he had never seen anything so terrible and that he would dream of it for the rest of his life.

[6] Reputedly they employed over 100 such.

[7] Operators who were nicked were supposed to receive a compensatory sum, paid to the wife, at so much a year for sentence, varying with the importance of their work. Sometimes it was paid, more usually it was bilked. The Krays were great bilkers and had done well out of the 'blue' films, shown in the less permissive fifties. The suppliers seldom got their money.

technique of the Nazi, who knows how to get away with it until it is too late.

The twins were now moving upwards fast. They had overtaken the Richardsons by the protection of innumerable small clubs, whose 'pension' was fixed on a percentage of the takings. They owned a clutch of clubs themselves and 'went social'. Photographs abound: there were a prodigious number of red faces when the Krays were ultimately nicked, though their known careers and earlier terms of imprisonment might have been thought to be a warning as to the results of association. Progress was interrupted by various attempts on the part of justice to lay hold of them: the story, supported by subsequent events, though clothed in secrecy at the time of writing, goes that they had dishonest police on their pay-roll. Certainly, both boasted on many occasions that they could not be taken, and they did, on one occasion, escape conviction for lack of hard evidence, a happening which informed people thought was odd. Eventually, a couple of murders, one so brutal that it must almost be a record in the annals of English crime, led to their arrest after concentrated work by Scotland Yard and to a trial unsurpassed for noise and impudence from the dock.

Heavy sentences, not only for the brothers but for their associates, had a salutary and instant effect on the rest of the underworld. Suddenly everyone was anxious to get himself in the clear and the stories that poured out about the doings of both gangs (no one feeling quite safe until everyone else was safely 'away') became almost boring in their quantity. The one that interested me most until I had checked on it was a rumour that the Krays had been about to start a drug-pushing racket in England (which was possibly true), organised with Cosa Nostra, which was about as likely as an alliance with the angels. American Mafia, as other English criminals have found to their cost, require loyalty and trustworthiness in their underlings and the Kray mentality was not one to commend itself there, nor could anyone imagine Kray megalomania taking orders. It is not impossible, however, that Cosa Nostra saw the chance of using them in some disposable way, such as making preliminary arrangements. Like many other cat's-paws, their usefulness at an end, they too would have been obliterated in the usual way. If an entirely objective view is taken of it, it seems almost a pity that American gangsterism was not left to deal with them, instead of having them cluttering up top-security wings of prisons entirely unsuited to dealing with psychopathic cases.[8]

I could have called this chapter 'The Richardson and Kray Phenomenon'. This is because, despite all the publicity that attended their activities and subsequent trials, they were something unusual in English criminal history. That violence is on the increase today is, as we have said, axiomatic; looking back over the years, mere inter-gang violence is not new at all. Rival mobs always fight and always will and Glasgow, for instance, is no Sunday school. But each of these two gangs had distinguishing features, the Richardsons intelligently conceived if lamentably executed financial ambitions, the Krays the attempt to introduce their own brand of American gangsterism into the English scene. Both gangs managed to become accepted by 'respectable' people: both got further than they might otherwise have done by means of corruption. Their eventual downfall (with the exception of one 'fixer' who fell with them) was popular amongst crooks: for a long time, at least, the underworld will be wary of any repetition that may harm themselves; and it is unlikely that, with a more efficient and more corruption-proofed police force, including a special 'gang-busting squad' created for the purpose, any similar gang will be able to take hold of so much control again. This is the belief of those members of the underworld whose views I respect; and one has only to listen to underworld talk to realise how vital to any progress in a war on crime a police force above reproach must be. Apart from anything

[8] Frequent threats come out of prison, I am told, mostly aimed at the relatives of anyone whom they dislike. Lip-service seems to be done by the 'faithful', but it is all really dead. An attempt to shoot a well-known figure who had fallen out with them, Charlie Mitchell (of horse-doping fame in the past), was attributed to them by the Press. It was not true: the shooting was the result of an alleged injury much nearer home. No damage was sustained by Mitchell and all simmered down. Since the Krays are rightly credited with many black deeds, it seems only fair to exonerate them on this one!

else, though the 'bent copper' may get information, it is the straight one who gets the most.[9] After all, who is going to put himself in jeopardy with a copper on whose word he cannot rely? Once bitten, twice shy. Twice bit, even more so.

[9] Far too many detectives have got into the habit of social and convivial meetings with underworld friends. Official policy is now cracking down on this and it looks as though the late J. Edgar Hoover's example in reforming the F.B.I. is going to be followed in the C.I.D.

Chapter 13

THE BUSY MONKEYS

The attitude of the underworld people to many everyday subjects is often exaggeration of normal reactions, sometimes easy, sometimes extremely difficult to explain. That towards violence, for instance, already considered in previous sections, is a case in point. Violence in the underworld springs normally from two causes : fear, either physical or from apprehension of being caught, whilst doing what the wrongdoer knows to be an act which the other world considers he ought not to be doing; and callousness, which is a good deal more prevalent in the underworld than in ours, though not so wholly as we should like to think. If one looks honestly at daily life, the actions of ordinary people do not always show quite the sensitivity to the sufferings of others that they might; and nothing grows on itself quicker than callousness. The abortion of a living foetus for instance, is a piece of gross violence even when justified. By the time a decent doctor or nurse has aborted fifty or so, does one imagine that a hardening process has not taken place? Whilst not an argument for or against what is, in its place, a necessary and grim service to the community, this deduction does emphasise the point that, just as in wartime, people become used to the sights after a night of bombing, so, whether it is abortion, coshing or bombs, a process of 'getting used to it' takes place in all mankind. *We* meet violence more often than we used to: the underworld are conditioned to it from birth.

A degree of schizophrenia is probably around in the underworld to an unsuspected degree. This condition, which is not the 'split-mind' of fiction but involves a measure of withdrawal from normal life, has, among its symptoms, an apparent inability in the sufferer to feel deeply about the things most people feel emotional about. There is generally also the formation of a sort of barrier to creating proper relationships with others.

These are precisely the symptoms one observes in the underworld. Again and again one notices the over-quick recovery from what might be thought to be almost mortal psychological blows. The cheerful acceptance of prison (very common), the even more cheerful taking up of life again might both be taken for courage, except that it happens rather too often. The crook's genuine devotion to home and family rarely extends to actually doing anything about them, except negatively, in that he is kind when he is about. But the underworld reaction to the loss of a wife or child gives one hard food for thought. I have known such a tragedy to strike many times. In the majority of cases (and there are many exceptions) the blow just does not seem to have the appalling impact which it does in the ordinary world. A 'good' funeral, the sympathy of friends, gracefully accepted, and within days everything is just as before, with the bereaved the heart and soul of the clubs and no 'professional' appointments deferred. Indeed, the main concern very often is the quality of the funeral. A good show here is a question of prestige and matters very much. It matters in other walks of life, but here it seems to be the end in itself, rather than incidental to it. What appeared on the surface to be a normal and deep relationship turns out to be something unbelievably shallow. Is there a lack of what used to be called 'proper feeling' here? If so, why and what causes it? If there is such a lack does it perhaps explain, without necessarily excusing it in any way, a certain insensitivity to the feelings of others?

The BBC once put on a programme in which Leslie Smith talked to three recidivists. Two were completely true to type, expressing rather feebly the desire to go straight, without any real drive behind the remark: in all probability, they were just trying vaguely to please, with what might have been a genuine feeling that it would be nice if they could keep out of the nick but not really probable. Both of them explained that they had no thought for their victims, and this was expressed not unkindly but with an air of surprise that anyone should think that they had. The victim was something impersonal, one explaining (almost like the respectable man who gets off the bus without paying because he is only robbing a 'company') that *he* 'would never rob a person' only 'things'. The third was salvageable. He was haunted by the injury he had done to a woman, from whose robbed handbang he had thrown away precious letters from a dead brother. He was the only one who was capable of personalising the victim and feeling shame and pity. 'Only financial – people get over that', was the remark of one of the others. This was real and accurate summing-up of a callousness which is all around one in the underworld. Yet years and years of knowing it have left me with the belief that this lack of feeling is not so much deliberate as something innate, almost in the chromosomes. Such a conclusion does not create in those who know it the desire to go 'soft' with criminals. It does, from time to time, engender a feeling of complete hopelessness and helplessness about the whole subject, unless and until we can get at our young criminals before anything happens and, in some way, penetrate the crust.

Underworld reactions tend to be superficial and somewhat like Kipling's Banderlog – the busy monkeys.

> 'Here we sit in a branchy row,
> Thinking of beautiful things we know,
> Dreaming of deeds that we mean to do,
> All complete in a minute or two –
> Something noble and grand and good,
> Won by merely wishing we could,
> Now we're going to – never mind,
> Brother, thy tail hangs down behind!'

And if, after all that, you add the chorus:

> 'Then join our leaping lines that scumfish through the pines
> That rocket by where, light and high, the wild grape swings,
> By the rubbish in our wake, and the noble noise we make,
> Be sure, be sure we're going to do some splendid things.'

you have pretty accurately described a lot of life in the underworld where grandiose schemes are brewed up every minute, where present thrills blot out all the future and where talk and more talk and still more talk goes endlessly on. Evidence is going to be produced to 'shake the Yard from top to bottom', another hero is about to 'bring off the biggest job in history', the certainty is that 'they'll never take *him*'. A fortnight afterwards, most of them do not even remember the big talk: there is some more anyway. Sometimes it is comical but there is something pathetically immature about it really. It is small boys' talk blown up. Perhaps this is the reason that so few women penetrate the (un) holy of (un) holies. It is not their way of life at all.

A degree of immaturity is no bar to a critical view of such members of the ordinary world as they come across. Their opinion of the Bar is tolerant, on the whole, ' 'Course, you can't expect them to know what's what' is a frequent somewhat pitying comment. Learned Counsel, to his client, is a simple kind of chap who has a special skill in one particular respect – his defence or, as it may be, his 'persecution' which is the frequent mispronunciation of 'prosecution' and possibly what they really mean. The underworld is not at all far out in this idea though learned Counsel are a bit more worldly[1] than they used to be and Judges no longer go much for judicial innocence. They know who The Beatles are these days.

Crooks do not like the Judges much. This is not so much because stiff sentences have been handed out to them but because of a belief that the judges interfere with parole prospects. 'I hear old So-and-So has spiked W's chances with the Board', is the sort of remark one hears. This is on a par with the belief which we shall meet again that the Judges are controlled by the police. Judges have seldom been popular, though on occasion, one or other has been responsible for reforming some individual; but over a period of years, there has always been a belief in some sort of conspiracy thought to be going on between Judges and

[1] Counsel are not in general credited with knowledge of the facts of life. One recently paid a kindly visit to a client, convicted and awaiting sentence. 'Why', said the barrister, 'don't you pack it in when you come out from this sentence. It would be better for you all round.' 'Pack it in!', replied the astonished prisoner. 'Why, I made more over this job alone than you make in a year! What would I be packing it in for?' Outstanding members of the criminal bar would, however, be astonished by the intimate details known about both their personal and professional qualities.

'someone', in which the Bench has played the part of a sneaky informer. Where this belief originated is obscure; but it is there and undefeatable.

Solicitors (with rare exceptions) and the 'Law' are reckoned to be 'no better than us', and it is no help to the police image that it is true that, socially, policemen and crooks come largely from the same social level. The solicitors that *are* 'better than us' are much feared, respected and mostly obeyed. There are few better arguments for the separation of Bar and solicitor in criminal practice than the different face shown by client to both. What the crook says to his solicitor has got to be said to someone and the solicitor is the first line of defence. It would be entirely impossible for an advocate to present the facts impersonally, truthfully and objectively if he had had to bear the brunt of the first impact of a scared, voluble and probably untruthful thief. There is often a familiarity between solicitor and client that some deplore. To me it is inevitable and not wholly a bad thing, unless it becomes unprofessional. Admittedly this is not unknown. It occurs mainly between managing clerks and clients rather than the heads of firms. The managing clerk is usually a person of great probity and many of them virtually run the business for the partners. But two facts make them more vulnerable. They do not have the professional training in ethics which the articled solicitor has and, if they stray over the borders of proper conduct, they do not face the penalty of being 'struck off'. Results can be serious. A prison break took place not so long ago with the assistance of a managing clerk (reputed to have received £5,000 for the job) whose carefully planned professional visits to the escapee dictated the timing of a successful escape. I imagine that the police know all about it, as it was a bit obvious in retrospect, but there was nothing whatever to be done about it. Managing clerks have also been known to help with the disposal of stolen money and there is a lot of bitterness over the extraction of 'fees' for so doing. Naturally, if someone who is part of a legal business does illegal transactions, he is not going to take an unprofitable risk. Diamond will cut diamond and disconsolate prisoners who think they have been 'robbed have been known to plan burglaries from inside prison, to even the score!

The underworld regard such crooked friends much as an African does a witch-doctor, though they reserve this particular description for the psychiatrists who cross their path, even ungratefully designating those who may try hard for acquittals as witch-doctor or head-shrinker. Few people like to be described as mentally unsound; and there is a rooted objection to allowing such a plea to go forward. The underworld has all the bourgeois distrust of qualified medical men and all the belief in the unorthodox, from osteopath to faith-healer. As unorthodox practitioners get more and more expensive, their clientele must be increasingly made up of a substantial majority of the dishonest, who are becoming the only ones who can afford their fees. Hypochondria is by no means unknown in these circles and, when surgical intervention is required, unorthodoxy flies out of the window, only the best is good enough and to hell with mistrust. Anyone who knows the underworld pays many, many visits to the private wings of the best hospitals, where, amid bowers of flowers, the invalid receives friends with tales from the great world, to the puzzlement of nurses who often find it somewhat difficult to place their patients' social surroundings. This cuts both ways. There are no friends more generous than the underworld, and, on the occasions when I have been at the receiving end of surgery, *my* room too has been a bower of flowers and *I* have never lacked visitors.[2]

Illness is rather a favourite topic with the underworld on the whole. Whether it is that such uses as a defence run on the lines of some obscure disease which is about to kill the defendant (but seems curiously unable to prevent him leaping over a bank-counter) popularises ill-health among them is doubtful: probably it is merely the same preoccupation with ill-health which marks the British as a whole: why the expression 'enjoys poor health'? Certain it is that no underworld character is ever at a loss for the 'best' specialist's name ('I tell you he took out Jacko's kidney without him knowing' has actually been said. 'Wonderful man – the most expensive man in Harley Street' was another doubtful recommendation) and many unknown ailments afflict the un-

[2] It occurs to me, however, that my funeral may lack some of the floral tributes expected, after all the hard things I have said in this book!

godly. When, at the Badger's, we are not discussing the wickedness of the 'Law', the redoubtable escape of some members, the unjust behaviour of a Judge or the run of luck, good or bad, of a friend, the talk often swings to the consideration of intimate details about a felonious inside. There is much drama here. Coronaries rarely seem to kill, strokes (fire from Heaven?) strike all right but the victim recovers: ulcers, after important and invariably expensive treatment, go away, perhaps because the underworld is self-employed and this state of affairs is well known to keep a man on his feet. Anything in the 'nutcase' line is reckoned to be good clean fun. The underworld is not at its nicest here. The helping hand which goes out to comrades in distress stops short of anything 'mental'. Perhaps this is further evidence of immaturity, fear seeming to be the reason behind it.

Chapter 14

SUPERSTITIONS DIE HARD

A great deal of gypsy blood runs in underworld veins, as many surnames there bear witness. This heritage may account for the fact that this world is intensely superstitious, to the extent that many a good burglary has been abandoned because something reckoned to be unlucky happened on the way.

Almost every wrong-doer has 'lucky' or 'unlucky' days, and many are the mascots carried.[1] One 'well-respected' thief cannot be persuaded into any venture on a Thursday. He has, he says, *proved* that it goes wrong and points to two nickings that happened. Sunday (just in case anyone thinks religion might have anything to do with it) is a distinctly lucky day for many, the best shop jobs taking place over the weekends! On the other hand, there was an Italian thief some years back who was both devout and dedicated to his craft. He always went to Mass before any secular activity such as shopbreaking and he had a regular system of hagiology of his own, having, apparently, worked out which Saint's Days were lucky for his particular interests. When the suggestion was made to him that, although the Roman Church had done a pretty good job in absorbing pagan deities and making them respectable, they had not, as far as is known, actually brought Mercury, patron saint of thieves, into good repute, he was vastly offended. He was intensely afraid of any dead object, being some sort of believer in voodoo, and I used to think that, if one knew where he was going to work, a dead bird on the doorstep would be quite sufficient to protect any house from his attention.

He was permanently cured by a shock of a kind unusual even in the underworld. He had been watching a house in a London

[1] The Krays are intensely superstitious. Born under Scorpio, they always wore their birth-sign amongst their other foibles and regularly consulted a fortune-teller.

suburb where there was some very pretty jewellery to be had. There was also a very pretty maid, together with whom he had hatched up a plan to rob the house when the couple who lived there were away for the weekend, and the maid would be alone. When he turned up at the appointed hour and waited around in the shrubbery, expecting a signal, he was rather surprised to find that all was quiet. Eventually he went to the front door and rang the bell with a carefully gloved hand and a glib enquiry ready if a stranger answered. Still no sound. After another interval he decided that they must have taken the maid with them and, the coast seeming clear, made his entry by a window with his usual skill and began to look round.

He knew that as well as the jewellery likely to be in the dressing-table drawers, a safe was concealed behind a picture in the downstairs cloakroom, a common device which used to be a good idea but no longer works, mainly owing to the camouflage pictures being so obvious – all similar pictures and all with the same heavy frames. He located the cloakroom, then, with a flashlamp, knowing that any passer-by could spot, if he happened to be looking, a light from the hall, put out his torch and crept across to the door. It was not locked but was unexpectedly heavy, seeming to be blocked by something placed against it. He pushed harder and the door swung back sharply, puzzling him, for he could not recollect seeing anything in the way before. On reflection, it occurred to him that a spring might have been fixed to close it automatically. What he could not explain was that something seemed to be swinging against the door. Suddenly he felt frightened. With his hair beginning to prickle, the thief opened the door against the weight sufficiently to get his head and hand round and switch on his torch for a fraction of a second. Then all caution abandoned, he was running across the darkened hall calling upon the Saints and switching on lights, without a thought except to find the quickest way out, for the obstacle was the dead body of the maid, hanging from a bar in the ceiling. I never heard the end of the story: I have always assumed that it was a suicide, probably because of pregnancy. One would have heard of it if it had been a murder.

Well, C never burgled again. He continued on a dishonest

course and did very well in different criminal activities, but never again did he venture inside other people's premises. One does not bump up against the corpse of one's girlfriend often, but the superstition against meeting something dead seems to be fairly common. It suggests gypsy or even African origins and is a bit reminiscent of voodoo: it has always interested me.

There is a widespread dislike of using the word 'rat'. There are thieves who will go to any lengths to avoid the use of the word or even forbid an outsider to use it in their presence. 'Four-legged gentleman', 'Him with a tail', 'Grey-waistcoated friend' and lots of other expressions are used. One must not even refer to someone 'ratting' on you and I got into real trouble on the first occasion I discovered the ban, which was through saying rather rudely 'Rats!' to some unusually silly piece of information, and had to work my way back into a position of trust after that. The idea is that it is an unlucky word, that its use brings disaster on an enterprise and that to see one moving when you are on a job means an almost certain 'nick'. It is tempting to trace this one back to some gypsy superstition (they are not very fond of the four-legged gentlemen either) but I have often wondered whether it does not originate in something more mundane. If you are 'screwing' away in a cellar where you ought not to be, the rats will obviously go away and keep quiet. But if the Law's heavy boots are on the trail, the rats will hear them and take fright before you do. It could possibly be this.

With superstition about, it is not surprising that much of the underworld reads the stars – or rather, the newspaper astrologers. Katina is top favourite. 'She's businesslike,' said P, who normally reads, as far as I know, only the racing pages. This taste seems to be shared by the financiers. They, we are told, also go by Katina. The seer does not, of course, mention whether such acquisitions of money as are spoken of are going to be your own – or other people's: burglaries advised by astrology are however quite common and are no more successful or unsuccessful than those which just 'happen'.

It is not necessary to go into the esoteric to find strongly held beliefs in the underworld. 'Michael' of Chapter 2 remarked: 'You couldn't beat some of these quaint ideas out of them.' The most widely held is that the police control the whole penal system and most of the world. This should interest the psychologists or perhaps the anthropologists. The man in blue who is at once all-powerful, to be placated with lavish gifts, who dominates life and is yet sometimes outwittable and endowed with human characteristics, may be just the Bogeyman of the nursery; but he bears a curious resemblance to the earthier gods of primitive society; and the underworld *is* primitive. What makes one feel that there is something very deep indeed here is the fanaticism with which they cling to the belief in police omnipotence, which has the irrational strength of something coming from deep down in the unconscious. The pundits may regard this as an extraordinary theory of mine. Failure to shift it in any way is even more extraordinary. It will take a lot to dislodge my theory out of me; and to this subject we shall return later in the chapter. For the moment there are one or two hopeful attempts at outwitting the police to pursue.

It used to puzzle me as to why so few members of the underworld were on the telephone. There have always been veritable 'exchanges', where the old crooks – by which one tends to mean those venerable figures who have reached fifty or so – kept their interest up and their hand in by living on the blower, when, that is, they were not gambling; for, 'When the enterprising burglar's not a'burgling' he is almost certainly a'gambling. I used to search the directory in vain when asked to get in touch with someone. Of course I ought to have known that they were all ex-directory and my private telephone book today is my most vital possession. Since every exchange has a list of its ex-directory numbers which can be obtained in certain conditions, it is childish to imagine that the police who know an address or even an approximate one have not got their own methods of tracing; though it is useless to try to persuade owners of ex-directory numbers that they are only brewing up trouble for themselves by making something mysterious out of the telephone.

Sometimes, indignation makes a caller throw all caution to the winds as when crises arise in this world, which is mostly in the small hours. Alas! that the day-worker acquaintance is considered to be on duty at the same time as the night-birds. About a quarter to two is a favourite time for the telephone bell to peal. Someone who has been drowning sorrow is on the other end. Threats of 'doing' the Judge 'He's got to go – there's nothing else for it', 'He'll be gone within two months – you wait and see' come over the wire followed by 'I tell you he's innocent. That boy never did it – all that bird and for something he never did. I'll get the IRA to get him if I don't do it myself' assail sleepy ears as the listener tries to shake himself awake, saying 'Who is it?' 'Never mind who it is' I was once told sharply in such a conversation; but had to listen to the end all the same. Things quieten down and no Judge has perished as yet; but it is a thought that one's position might be awkward if that Judge *did* get 'done'.[2]

Telephone calls with the underworld follow a fairly usual pattern. To begin with, names are never used. It takes a bit of practice to identify voices which are all too similar in intonation and, on more than one occasion, I have conducted quite a conversation with what I took to be A only to discover that it was B. The idea is, as may be imagined, to put the hounds off the scent. Everyone also imagines his line to be bugged, as I have said before. The theory is that if a converation is started about some entirely neutral subject, the listening Scotland Yard will lose interest. So opening gambits tend to delay matters with prolonged inquiries about health, holidays, behaviour of children and animals and such small talk, all remarkably odd chatter for 2 a.m. Eventually, we arrive at the meat. This tends to be punctuated with suspicious remarks such as 'Did you hear that click? They're changing the tape – we'd better talk another time' – words calculated to put any sleuth on the alert. But excitement or emotion triumph ere long. Soon the wildest indiscretions are being committed – by them. Woe betide if the respectable end of the

[2] There was a slightly embarrassing episode once over a trusted and most honourable friend who had been head of the foreign department at my bank. When he retired, we asked him in to have a drink and, over a convivial glass, he told us that he was going to a responsible advisory post with a merchant bank. I laughed and said, 'Oh, I'll have you bound and gagged and your bank cleaned out within a fortnight.' It was just a fortnight later that his merchant bank was raided, he and all the others on the premises at that time being bound and gagged! One was always told in the nursery that many a true word was spoken in jest.

conversation oversteps the mark. 'You didn't ought to say that' admonishes me from time to time, though I am far more cautious than they are, not wishing to become involved in any dubious knowledge.

One very old friend, long since reformed but still 'free' of the community, mocks the unwise conversation accurately. 'Hullo', says the voice at the other end, 'It's me. I must see you – urgent.' 'Yes', says my friend, 'Where?' 'Same bar', says the voice, 'You know, the one behind Marble Arch. Same time as usual, Sunday – all the boys will be there.' 'I don't think I can make it', says the reformed one, not at all anxious to be involved but willing to help none the less. 'You must', says a voice at the other end, 'It's urgent. It's about those' (here there is a pause, the speaker evidently realising that he is not being as careful as he might be), 'Well, you know, those things what I told you about.' As the conversations almost always originate in a 'job' which is interesting to the police, it is small wonder that those who indulge in them manage to bring down wrath on their heads. Some telephone lines *are* a bit hot!

The subject of police omnipotence was well discussed one evening in the Badger's. Most journalists are used to arguing from a minority angle but I have seldom fought so hopeless a battle or from such an isolated position. No one believed me: no one appeared even to *want* to believe me and the idea that having been born and bred in legal circles might possibly have given me some knowledge of the way things were conducted was laughed to scorn. 'Conned you they have', said old Alf, always the sage of the club, 'Same as they do the others.'

The actual topic that had fired off the argument was the thirty-year sentences imposed upon the Mail-Train robbers. I had been quite happily going with the majority verdict that it was unbelievably severe and also unlikely to deter anyone else if they saw an equally good chance when, hardly crediting my ears, I heard the Badger remark that 'Of course Edmund Davies' (thus familiarly do the victims speak of the Judges who sentence them) 'had to take his time from old Butler.' ('Old Butler', who died tragically almost immediately on his retirement, was 'Tommy' Butler, head of the Flying Squad and mainly responsible for the pursuit and subsequent arrest of the actors in this drama. He was at times spoken of with the utmost loathing and at others with great respect, on the grounds that he might be a swine but never took money – not that that is always a feature that commends itself to the hopeful.) I roared with laughter, only to discover that my mirth was not being communicated to the others, who clearly thought I had taken leave of my senses. 'You don't know *that*!' came the chorus. 'Of course the Judge fixes it up with the Law first. How do you think he knows what to hand out?' 'I tell you', said Ginger, 'I had it from a Super that Butler made Edmund Davies promise thirty-year sentences first or the Law would never have gone into the box.'

I began to attempt to explain the judicial system in simple terms, pointing out that Judge, jury (not such strong ground perhaps at a time when the corruption of jurors was being attempted hot and strong) not to mention Counsel, were all completely separate entities and that the suggestion that police officers had any contact with – let alone influence upon – a High Court Judge, was so lamentably silly that it was just not a subject for serious discussion. (I had already on previous occasions tried to dispel the parole myth, mentioned in an earlier chapter, but without success.) Who, I asked, had ever seen a cop walking up to the Judges' Lodgings? Didn't they know the awe and majesty of the Bench: did they imagine that the cops, whom they had frequently described to me as no better than themselves (socially, I mean), could possibly sit cheek by jowl with the said figures of awe and majesty and brew up sentences? 'They could use the blower', said Frank with conviction. 'That's easily fixed. You don't have to show your face on a job like that.' Pitying murmurs about innocence, the fact that I had been 'around so long and don't know *that*' were all too audible. 'What about my husband?', I asked. 'Do you suppose *he* wouldn't know if this sort of thing went on?' At this, Terry, youngest of the villains present, informed us that he had a cousin, who worked in the Post Office telephones as an engineer who could give you his oath that he heard a Judge (name not disclosed) talking to a police-superintendent (Well, he 'thought it must be a Super') about the correct sentence to give in another case. Murmurs of applause and much head-nodding. I knew I should never break this one down, so merely suggested that what the engineer overheard was someone placing a bet under a pseudonym. This was not well received.

I gave up and, some days later, approached an extremely intelligent and well-informed member of the fraternity and asked if this business about police was a widely held view. To my amazement, he was similarly astonished that I had not picked it up before. Of *course* the police told the Judge what to do, he said – and seemed to think that it was almost a good idea. (Perhaps any money paid as bribe is supposed to get through to altogether higher things!) 'But doesn't it strike you as strange', I asked him, 'that no member of the Bar knows anything about this.' 'Ah', said Lou, 'they don't tell them till they get up there. Then they find out what's what. 'Course they have to come into line – the Law wouldn't work otherwise. They'd probably go on strike and then, where would you be.'

This incredible story has many variations. I have before me at this moment a letter from prison, dealing with a well-known prisoner's prospects for parole. So far as Judges are concerned, he is confident that, personally, they might well support his application. He is terrified that the police will be able to hold this up: he is satisfied (though having great faith in my judgement on other matters) that I just don't understand what he *knows* to be correct – that his removal to a more convenient prison (which has happened to others convicted of the same crime) has been forbidden by the police and is right out of the hands of the Home Office. Like many another prisoner, he is by now almost suffering from delusions of persecution.[8]

Once this underworld belief is appreciated, it is much easier to understand why so much police bribery is attempted. The whole thing remains, I think, extremely interesting. If the primi-

[8] One's attempts to defeat this belief and to instil some sense of the justness of justice are admittedly not helped by Home Office procedures. The evasions, the buckpassing and the inefficiency of that overloaded department have been the despair of the Press for a long time. It takes the detailed knowledge that comes by the following-up of individual prisoners' fates to turn anyone who wishes to encourage the moral re-habilitation of a prisoner into a sour 'bolshie', intent only upon bringing down the 'Men from the Ministry' in flames. The pity of it is that they are all so well-meaning. Well, the road to hell has been paved that way for some time.

tive sub-culture that knows itself as an entity and lives by preying on others is a throwback to a much earlier stage in man's history, which is a theory held by some criminologists – this is a piece of corroboration, though the wide boys would be vastly offended if I put this view to them. *Primitive* indeed!

Chapter 15

LAUGHING TO THE BANK

Full understanding of any foreign terrain comes with the ability to understand its humour, and it is certainly true of the underworld that what is funny there throws a lot of light on attitudes in general. Underworld humour is primarily that of the social class from which it originates. But there is a sting in the tail more often than in normal slapstick. If the psychologists are right in saying that we laugh at those things which we fear most, its preoccupation with jokes about things going wrong is easily understood. An awful lot of things go wrong when you spend your days doing things you should not. Humour in these circles is uncomplicated too. It is a naïve world: the ability of these striving conners to be conned is perennial and the majority of underworld inhabitants, whatever their morals, are fairly simple souls in essentials. They like Alf Garnett (but only at his face-value); they love Steptoe and Son, which they consider real life; old Chaplin films; Laurel and Hardy and many other classical examples of tragi-comic little men getting into extraordinary situations have them rolling in the aisles, young and old. Satire passes them by, with rare exceptions, and sarcasm is abhorred by one and all. I once had a big and unpremeditated success by saying something reminded me of 'Bird thou never wert'. My hearer couldn't stop giggling and kept on saying to all comers 'She says some poet said "Bird thou never wert." Why don't you try it on the missis – I'm going to' and then relapsing into further giggles, exactly like an eight-year-old who has picked up some choice bit of silliness.

Prison humour is very black. It is frequently very funny too, but the macabre streak that runs through it betokens a bad-dream quality which gives one furiously to think. The house-magazines that emanate from gaol feature short stories which combine sadism and masochism in large doses. Prison also brings out crude sex-humour – understandably – generally with a sadistic streak in it: with the exception of the mildest of schoolboy vulgarity, I have seldom heard much of this in, say Badger's. This restraint is undoubtedly due to my own sex; but such protection is not afforded women in Fleet Street!

One reason that anybody familiar with underworld circles is liable to be accused of finding crime amusing (quite unjustly in general) is that many funny stories abound there. Cheerfulness is normal there anyway; far too much sometimes; and listeners, like children demanding the familiar, never tire of such stories as the mishaps of the burglars who intended a break-in in Green Street, Mayfair.

It was, says legend, a well-cased job. The butler (previous history including prison) had been squared and had provided perfect keys on the understanding that he got a generous 'cut'. Everything was laid on as cautiously two of the band approached the house, leaving the driver in the car round the next corner, put the key in the lock and turned it. As the door began to open, they saw two men peering round the corner of the curved staircase at them. They closed the door quickly and retreated round the corner to the escape-car, ready for flight, but nothing happened. This was very puzzling, so, after half-an-hour's wait, they returned and tried again. Again the silent watchers glided into view. Thoroughly terrified and by now imagining supernatural interference, all three repaired to drink and the whole plan was abandoned. It was a week later that they ran their accomplice to earth and discovered that what they had seen was a mirror on the stairs, reflecting their own image. But by this time, the butler had had the sack and the locks had been changed. Since everyone has had many a let-down on the job, this story is much appreciated and never fails to raise a laugh.

Another old chestnut, popular with the younger generation, concerns a well-known member of the underworld who, not so many years ago, formed one of an assault-party of three who had had their eyes for some time on a high-class furrier – another 'good' Mayfair job. They had got inside and begun work when one of them, looking out of a window, saw a couple of Squad cars drawing up outside. One thief went up the water pipe, another through the skylight. The third, plump of build and no athlete, took the only other route. He fled down to the basement, thinking that he might perhaps get out that way. The back door however was locked. Looking round in desperation he saw a cleaner's overall and some strong-lensed spectacles. He donned the lot and pulling his cap down over his forehead, he seized a tall feather-duster from the cleaner's pile and almost unable to see through the lenses, made for the front door, through which the Flying Squad had entered the building and had begun to search. The ridiculous feather object in his hand, he started a diligent dusting of the glass facia-board outside the premises and, after a moment or two, moved gently towards the next house, the feather duster still at the ready. Gradually, he reached the corner of Grosvenor Square and, once round it, snatched off the spectacles and broke into a brisk walk which rose to a quick trot as he reached Oxford Street. There, by Selfridges, he parked the feather-duster against a lamp-post and leapt on to the first bus, only to be pursued by the duster, assiduously following him by the courtesy of a zealous fellow passenger.

There is a decent respect for copyright in the underworld. Whatever they do steal, a non-stop process on the whole, they do not pinch one another's stories. Which is as well, because there is never any lack of anecdote there. Like Henry V's men at Agincourt, the thief 'remembers with advantage what feats he did this day'. When the underworld foregathers, at the club or round the family hearth, talk is often of the great deeds (most certainly remembered with advantage) and, among the raconteurs, old and young, there are some who vie with the *spielman* of Scandinavian legends for the length and complexity of the sagas they relate.

I have always been a complete sucker for stories told or read aloud. I wait avidly for a new 'Book at Bedtime' almost as keenly as I demanded 'Tell me a story' in nursery days. So I genuinely enjoy the underworld anecdote. There is a hypnotic quality about it, for, whether told by young or old, it conforms to the same ritual, told invariably in the present tense, slightly mimed and subject to a saga-like tendency to repetition.

As with the rest of us, dismal things get forgotten and, since adventure and comradeship form a genuine, if distorted, part of the illegal life, the teller tends to work for a laugh by the glorification of old Charlie or young Tom. Terrible things happen in the underworld; but it is, after all, part of life which goes on and has always done so and there is a funny side to many misfortunes. I have tried to record two stories which amused me for their differing qualities. The first told by an intelligent and experienced 'pro' in his thirties is pure Runyon. Damon Runyon knew his world: allowing for pardonable extra craftsmanship and making ends tie up neatly, he could have depicted life in the Badger's club without any trouble whatever in changing styles. This tale of the successful outwitting of diligent police, edited as little as possible, is considered the funniest happening for a number of years by the club connoisseurs: its particular piquancy is imparted by the fact that, for once, the Law was completely scored off, without more than a reasonable and expected comeback. In the game of cops and robbers, played by all the fraternity, a draw is an honourable conclusion of the game. I doubt its truth, but something of the sort certainly happened.

The second is the story of the most tragi-comic Christmas ever spent by one of my best underworld friends of more than twenty years' standing, long since reformed. It contains quite a bit of underworld reasoning and here I have had to rely on voluminous notes as the tape broke down; and no story-teller can be at his best when he has to do the whole thing over again stone-cold; so we went on as we were. There is a generation-gap between the two stories but there is a firm continuity of pattern between them, though the actual style of anecdote is different. The rueful acceptance of fate is identical – and so is the total amorality. In fact, the two stories illustrate underworld attitudes better than a commentator can do.

Imagine therefore, the modern setting for the *spielman*. The Badger's is comfortably full: the haze of expensive cigar-smoke rises around the well-filled glasses (was that excellent whisky actually bought?), old Alf who has heard the story before (as most of us have) is snoozing down over his bitter, though ready to wake and correct any error or undue interpolation, and the rest of us are plying Terry with enough lubricant for the larynx to ensure our money's worth. Crossing elegantly clad, tightly-trousered legs, the story-teller begins.

'We was all sitting around, like it might be now, when in rushes Ginger, looking like the Flies[1] was on his heels. He sits down and yells for Badger and the strongest drink he's got and we all gather round to see what has taken him, "It's the Sarti ring",[2] says Ginger when he's got his breath back. "The law had it last night and they'll be on to me before the day's out. I daren't go home and I daren't phone the wife. What the hell am I to do?" Ginger puts his hand in his pocket and pulls out a packet and there, as solid as you like, is the Sarti ring. I reckon I must be seeing things, because hasn't Ginger just said that the law had it, in which case, what is it doing in his pocket?

'Ginger says that he was nicked last night for being drunk in charge. The nicking took place in the country, where Ginger had a beautiful job in mind, screwing a house with Flasher – you know him – does buttling jobs and always gets trusted with the keys. Ginger had bought the ring off him after the big job and we thought he must have had a good home for it, for it never occurred to anyone that he would be such a mug as to keep it around. But Ginger is always an odd one and he didn't dare leave it around for his missus to find, so it is on him when he is nicked.

' "How come the law to give it you back?" says Ferdie. Ferdie, you know him, asks questions like some briefs, who've got nothing better to do, so asking awkward questions is a habit with them, like the law, though not so spiteful. Ginger says it just shows. He was nicked by a kid law and Ginger finds, to his surprise, that his name don't mean anything at all to the law, no more to the sergeant, very bored, who lists the contents of his pockets whilst Ginger is sobering up in the cells. Ginger is almost too surprised by this to think up a yarn but he pulls himself together and pitches a sob about how he'd saved up for

[1] The Flying Squad from Scotland Yard.

[2] The name Sarti has no significance. It is the name of my good friend who owns the Chateau de Madrid at Villefranche and who, as well as producing exquisite food for me, never minds his name being taken in vain for a good cause.

years to buy the greatest present ever for his little girl's wedding and how he's been so worried by the whole thing that he has just had a drink too much. As what he's got on his mind is whether Flasher would do him down over the job they've just done, he doesn't have much trouble looking worried and so, when the doc. says he's sober, they let him go so long as he turns up at the Court and he bolts back to the smoke,[3] knowing that when the description of the ring is checked up, he's for the high jump.

'Well, there it is and no one can think what to do and one or two aren't even very keen on Ginger being around, on account of the law perhaps looking for him in the club, so there's a bit of a clearout and the rest of us sit around and promise to visit him in the nick and keep an eye on his missus and the dishy Miss Ginger, when suddenly Ferdie lets out a yell. "Why don't we find Jacko", he says, his eyes shining like that day he backed an accumulator and it came up. "Why don't we do what, you big sap?" says Badger, "Jacko isn't interested since he took up with that bird – not that that'll last long." Ferdie smiles more and more and rubs his hands together. "Why shouldn't Jacko make a ring", he says, "A beautiful ring, just like this one, with a receipt and a number on it. Only it won't be the Sarti ring, but one that maybe they think the Sarti dame is going to swing on the insurance."

'That's all right, except it comes to me that the only person who is going to work Jacko is me, us being old mates and Jacko's bird still liking me which is more than she does any of the others of his gang. I don't want to be involved, so I make for the toilet which is on the way out. But Ginger follows me. "You can't run out on me, Terry", he says, "Go round and pressurise Jacko, do. It's my only chance. Here's the ring."

'It takes me a fair time to find Jacko, since I avoid a lot of streets and that blessed ring feels like it's white-hot, which it is, in a manner of speaking. But the law hasn't got anything on me at the moment, not that you can trust them, and by luck, Jacko is in, lounging about watching TV in a knocked-off silk dressing-gown, whilst the bird, who has got a goddam awful sort of bird's

[3] 'Smoke – London.

nest of bright red hair up top is weaving around in a shimmery trouser-suit. She gives a scream and puts on dark glasses, because she says she looks a fright, which is true. I say that I have come on business and Jacko looks happy and tells the bird to scram. Jacko looks real pleased to see me, us being old pals from juvenile delinquents together. So I tell him about Ginger's trouble and there is a real nasty smile about him but all he says is, "It'll cost, you know." The bird puts her head round the door at this point and Jacko tells her to belt up pretty sharp, as he has important business. Then he says that it is okay and Ginger is not to worry at all. He will simply keep the ring. This is not at all what Ginger is thinking and I am not at all keen on taking the news back to him but Ginger is in no position to choose. Jacko only says nastily, "He did me down over that hi-jacking last year and justice is justice, Terry, and everyone has got to see it done, like what that Judge said to Alf."

'Well, Ginger is up the pole and if there is one thing about Jacko it is that he is reliable. So I go back to the Badger's with the news that someone had better break it to Ginger that it is okay but he is not going to win out on the price. Ginger is hiding up with a sister-in-law, one of those sour-faced cows who will give you a hand if necessary rather than muck up the family name with another apples and pears[4] at the Old Bailey. Badger says that the Flies have been and turned Ginger's house over and that what Miss Ginger said to the Inspector was enough to make one of the young tecs leave the room quick. Ginger is much too fly to keep anything hot, so the Squad have had no end of a search for nothing and are in a bad mood. As we all know the performance Mrs G. can put on when her house is turned over, we are just having a good laugh when the Flies decide to pay us a visit.

' "Come right in, Inspector", says Badger, using his loaf to slow things up so as Freddie, in the kitchen, can put the drinks into a plastic bucket. "I suppose you've got a search-warrant. Perhaps I can see it. Nothing personal, of course, just to keep things regular. Nothing for you here, but you're always welcome." The Inspector is used to Badger and knows when he is beat. "I'm

[4] Rhyming slang for 'stairs' the stairs from dock to cells.

just paying a routine call", he says, "in the hope of picking up Ginger Higgins. I suppose he isn't around here." "Inspector", says Badger, "you know me too well to think I should deceive the police. I haven't seen Ginger for a week so help me. And if he's in trouble, I don't want him here. This is a respectable club and that's how I want to keep it."

'The Inspector sniffs and takes a look round but there is nothing he can do so he goes away after peering into the kitchen where Freddie is busy with the washing-up and Badger thanks his lucky stars that the Inspector's got a cold or he might have noticed the smell from the bucket. Soon after that, Ginger comes in as angry as angry which you can see by the way his hair's standing on end. "Anyone going to drive me home", he says. There isn't exactly a rush, because everyone is thinking of the Squad cars waiting outside his house and you can't trust the law. "I should think Terry's planning his South American holiday" he says, "after the way he's sold me down the river." "No need to talk like that", says Badger, "we all know you've had a scare but Terry here done his best for you." "We've had the Flies here too", says Ferdie, "and Badger don't want no more trouble."

' "All right", says Ginger, "but it burns me up to think of Jacko sitting pretty with that lot. Not but what he's done a beautiful job with this", he adds, pulling the fake out of his pocket and a lovely job it is alright. Ferdie bursts out laughing, slaps Ginger on the back and says "Okay, boy. I'll drive you home. I want to see the blushes when the truth, the whole truth and nothing but the truth dawns upon the rozzers." "Very old-fashioned in your talk, aren't you Ferdie?"

'Ferdie turns up with Ginger and sure enough the Flies pounce on him like he was bad meat. "Henry Higgins", says the Inspector, "I have a warrant for your arrest for being in unlawful possession of a ring recently stolen." Then he cautions him. "Stolen, Inspector", says Ginger. "I deny everything. This here ring is what I bought in Kingston Market from a man what I never saw before, as a present for my little girl here, when her Mr Right comes along." Then the women go off like they were those peacocks what got us done last year when we was down near Ascot and Ginger turns to the Inspector and says, "You can take me away and hang me if you like, but take me away from these here mad females before I go round the bend myself."

'Well, course, when the law gets to the shop it turns out that it isn't the Sarti ring at all and it's those fake sparklers which you take the mugs in with, not real rocks at all, so they have to let Ginger go. But Nobby's cousin who works in Hatton Garden says she hears there was no end of a barney over it, as the jeweller was a lot under-insured and what with that and the idea that they got that it had been a switch to do the insurance, nobody bothered over Ginger any more. But they got Jacko. He went and gave the bird the big ruby out of the ring when he's broken it up, because he said the fences offered him such diabolically low money. She goes and flashes it about in the supermarket, like he told her not to and the old hand comes down on her shoulder and being new to the game, she's given it all away before she's reached the station. Ginger's inside now, nicked on a job a kid could do, and the laugh of it is they've fetched up in the same nick, so I reckon they've patched it up. You can't win, can you?'

The second story is different and depicts a less-assured underworld. Tommy has become a sage and elder and, living a godly, upright and sober life but never forsaking his friends, has retained the respect and affection of all. He has not done badly for himself, despite many a knock from cruel fortune and false friends; he is the confidant and counsel of young and old alike and moves in influential circles. But although he loves and is proud of his successful breakaway from crime, his eye still lights up at the thought of the days when he was a name with which to conjure in the underworld, when he made headlines in the 'Sundays', jumped his bail to Australia, sending back the money for his guarantor (for Tommy was always a gentleman) and saw, through his porthole, an Arab rescue armada – setting out from Marseilles, ready to storm the ship bearing him back to captivity – foiled, and so preventing him from becoming an epic of the underworld which would indeed never be forgotten!

'In those days', said Tommy, 'you couldn't trust the law like you can now. I'd been nicked a few days before Christmas but the Inspector had given me his word that he'd leave me alone till the New Year, 'cos he knew I'd give myself up. Course, I had to give him something but that's fair enough.

'Well, I was feeling at peace with the world. It was one of those cold Christmases and the wife had got a good fire going. The kids had gone off to the aunt while we finished the decorations and the rest and I was just plucking the turkey. A beauty it was too. Knocked off? Yes, course it was. Farmers are a cheating lot and my pal reckoned that one would even the scores a bit.

'Suddenly, the wife rushes in. She's all covered with the stuffing. Do you like stuffing – I always think it's the best part of the bird. "Tommy", she says, "there's two Squad cars outside. Look for yourself. That Inspector's a crook! I told you so!" Sure enough, there are. Old B is just getting out of one. "For God's sake", I say, "give me three minutes. Bolt the door and be a long time answering." So I bolt upstairs and then I remember. "And don't forget the Christmas present", I whisper to her, over the banisters. The wife does all right. She puts her hand to her blouse and picks off the brooch I'd got her. She stuffs it into the turkey's middle and then she goes to the door, where the old "Open up" is going on. "Who is it?" she keeps on saying, until the Law, getting impatient, begins to tell her what was going to happen if she didn't get a move on. She keeps it up for close on five minutes before she lets them in, saying that there had been such a lot of funny things in that neighbourhood that you couldn't be too careful. I can hear old B who doesn't seem too pleased. "Where is he?" he says, "I know he's here because we've been watching the premises. Tell him to come down and I'll make it easy for him."

'Meanwhile, of course, I'm in the airing-cupboard. A friend of mine did the job for me and he's a beautiful worker, so there isn't a trace of the hiding-place, which you get into at the back and then work your way up under the floor of the loft. Take a mine-detector to sniff you out and they didn't use dogs in those days. Just a false panel, but nothing to make you suspicious. I noticed the space when I took the house and thought it might come in useful.

'I can hear them scratching about all over the place and once old B uses some language when he hits his head on the kitchen shelf. The wife is letting off at them proper, telling them what she thinks of the mess they're making and old B is in a proper paddy too. "No use telling me he isn't here", he keeps on saying. "I'll find him if I have to tear the place apart." "Just what you are doing", says the wife, "with your great flat feet all over my nice, clean place what I've just cleaned up for Christmas. I'll go to your Superintendent, I will. I've told you he cleared out early today and I haven't the least idea where he is." "That's a likely story", says old B. "I'm staying around till I find him, so you can put that in your Christmas turkey and like it." The wife keeps her pecker up and presently, I hear them in the bathroom and I fairly say my prayers. But even when they poke around the airing cupboard, no one spots the panel, though I have a bad minute when one of the nosey youngsters taps it. Then they go away.

'It's very cramped in the hole and cold enough to freeze you. I forgot to tell you it was one of the coldest Christmases we've had and there isn't a speck of heat in my hideout. I am cursing the fact that I never thought of that, when it occurs to me that they'll go away soon so I say to myself, "Buck up, Tommy. It'll be Christmas dinner before long." I hear the front door slam and wonder why the wife doesn't come up, till I hear a cough from the kitchen and then the wife's voice in the hall, "Make yourself at home, I'm sure. The kids will be back soon and", she says, raising her voice, "don't hesitate to go upstairs and search it all over again. You've made so much mess it'll make no difference. And if you want the toilet, by all mean use ours upstairs. Can't expect the law to go down the yard." So I know that the law is sitting in the kitchen and that's Em's way of tipping me off. I also know that the law won't come upstairs after that.

'I tell you, Peta, I've felt sorry for mice ever since. I know just what the little beggars feel like with the cat sitting watching the hole. But I sit there, still feeling that it can't last, the law will soon get sick of it. So the kids come home and ask for Daddy. I slide the panel a crack and hear the law trying to be uncle-like and it makes me feel madder than ever. I'm getting stiff with cold. It's dark outside and I can hear the roof making cracking noises with the frost. But still the law doesn't budge.

'The kids are making the hell of a noise now and Em comes up to the toilet and whispers round the bathroom door that she reckons the law is going to stick around for a bit longer but that he'll slope off last thing. I say can't she get me some grub and she says how can she, with the law around. So I try to slide the panel an inch or two and the damn thing sticks. Now there's no getting it open except from the outside and that's out of the question with the law about.

'I can hear a clock somewhere but can't make out what it is striking. Then I hear the law going out, saying, "Well, I can't really wish you a happy Christmas in the circs but if your old man turns up, at least we'll be able to leave you in peace." The girl sets up a howl at this, crying "I want my Daddy, Father Christmas won't come if he's not here", and I feel real miserable. Presently Em comes upstairs. "It's no good, Tommy", she says, "the Squad car's outside and another has just taken over. They reckon you'll come home for Christmas if you're not in the house. They've taken the curtains down in the front room, so as they can keep an eye on it. I don't know what we can do, but I'll bring you some supper when I've got a chance."

'But she can't get it to me because it'll take a carpenter to open that panel. If she goes out and fetches a pal, the law will want to know what she's doing and she daren't use the blower, 'cos you know what the law are. Anyway, who's going to stick his neck out when there's a Squad car outside. I say some things about old B out loud to myself. Miserable old sod, if you'll pardon the expression, and after taking the money too. So I've just got to stick tight. Em daren't come often in case the kids get nosey.

'I go to sleep and wake wondering what the first symptoms of pneumonia are. I have a fit of sneezing too, on account of the dust really, but I thank my stars it didn't happen when the law was looking round. Then I smell the turkey cooking and it nearly drives me mad. Great wafts of it come up. I explore a bit and get into the roof rafters. The doorbell rings and Em shouts "Oh, it's you again. Can't you find nothing better to do than persecute an innocent woman – on Christmas Day too!" I hope she doesn't offer him that turkey but I don't reckon Em would give him anything without the arsenic in it just now.

' "Innocent woman, is it?" he says from the hall. "If you want to know what Tommy's wanted for, it's a brooch he nicked last week. We got the whisper that he's had it among a lot he fenced but he didn't want to part with it for some reason or other. We think it might have been a coincidence that you had a birthday two days ago. He's a good husband, Tommy, isn't he, if he didn't have to leave you quite so often." So I know Sammy the fence has shopped me and I think what I will do to him.

'Em must have turned pale but I must say she puts on a wonderful act. The law must be glad he'd got reinforcements outside and he's soon saying, "There, there. Mustn't get upset. We've got our work to do the same as you. I'm sorry if I hurt your feelings but you can work it all off on Tommy when he shows up. "Not", he adds, "that you'll be seeing much of him for a bit." That starts the waterworks off again when suddenly the girl calls from the kitchen, "Mum, Mum, the turkey's burning!"

'The long and short of it is that the law, would you believe it, gets his dinner with them. Enough to give you a stroke. But I have to wait till afterwards for Em to tell me the squeak she has. It seems the law is not very hungry. "I'll just have a little of the stuffing", says he. Em has to think quick. She gets the spoon and tastes it, then she shakes her head, "I *knew* that butcher done me over the sausage-meat", she says. "Sour, that's what it is!" The law looks disappointed but Em is quite firm. "I daren't let you have it", she says hard as nails. "As if it wasn't bad enough to have my husband on a charge without poisoning the police. What do you think they'd make of that. Hang us both, as like as not. No, officer, you can have another slice of breast but no one – no one is going to touch that stuffing." The boy pipes up, "Mum, the sausage is at the other end. It's Paxo in the front end, you know it is." Em fetches him a swipe with the spoon and tells him to belt up. "Who done the cooking", she asks, "not you, Master Knowall." The law says he must be a good boy and wait for the pudding and Em gets the turkey out into the kitchen, just in time, 'cos the brooch has shifted and she can see a shiny bit beginning to show through.

'I can tell you I'm near crying by this time. It was after six that they give up and slope off. Em watches until she is sure the coast is clear and then she comes up and asks me what to do. I feel like telling her to get a chopper and break it down, because I know that the catch has broken and nothing but brute force is going to shift it without a man that knows it but it seems a pity, after all that, to give in, and I might need it again, so I tell her to get hold of Bert, which means a bus ride and bring him along. But for Pete's sake to see the coast is clear before he gets near the house as he's wanted too. She gets him and he opens it. But he's no pal for he's laughing so much that he can't stand up when I creep out. "Good as the pictures", he says between bursts. I'm so mad, I just have a meal and then scarper and go missing for a fortnight, instead of surrendering like I'd promised old B. When I walk into the station, he looks surprised to see me. "Where were you, Tommy?" he says. I look back at him and smile. "Somewhere where you don't know about", I say. "Somewhere very private indeed." He looks sour and says "We know you've got that brooch, Tommy. Why don't you give it up and make it easy for yourself." "Now you're talking turkey, Inspector", I says. "Only I don't happen to know its whereabouts." He don't know what I'm talking about.'

Chapter 16

CHRISTMAS–WITH A DIFFERENCE

It is in the common festivities of life that common humanity is most apparent. If the moral approach to such enjoyments is not identical, well, one would hardly know it, unless you happened to be nosey enough to make too many inquiries. Take the underworld celebration of Christmas. Christmas is Christmas in the underworld – a time for gentlemen to rest and to be merry. This is the season when a truce is observed between the law and the crook, much as between rival armies in the field.[1] A good deal of hard bargaining goes on before the villain, who is wanted for a particular piece of villainy, can feel assured that he will not be taken until after the Christmas season; and delicate angling for position also goes on. One underworld cynic used to knock off sufficient Scotch early in the year to enable the dispensing of largesse at the Christmas season. This was not done crudely: he did not present bottles to the relevant members of the police force, but instead a certain number were donated for the kiddies' parties. Wonderful what those police kiddies drink! Mysterious turnings-in of stolen property are not unknown; intermediaries abound and many a pathetic story is put up as to the beneficial results of a few more days' freedom at Christmas. On the whole the system works pretty well, the interests of justice are not thwarted in the end, and an uncertain peace hangs over the underworld for a few days.

For the underworld is great on Christmas. One should expect this: they are one of the last pillars of tradition in the country, and firmly opposed to any innovation which does not contribute directly to their income. Their timing is a little different from ours. Christmas is condensed to a higher intensity: business is,

[1] The result of the Inspector's faithlessness in the matter of Tommy was that it was a long time before any crook vouchsafed information to 'old B' again.

after all, business, and there are too many good pickings to be had from careless people on Christmas Eve and torpid people on Boxing Day to prolong the festive season overmuch. There are also points of honour to be observed. A high-class operator likes to give high-class presents; but there is no point in being silly and actually paying good money for what you can get in any other way. One well-known screwsman has been noted for some thirty years for his generosity in Christmas presents. He has never failed to surprise his friends by the novelty of these presents and they have never cost him a penny. His method is quite simple. It is to obtain the name of someone who has an account at one of the good shops and is known to be going away for Christmas. He then rings up the shop (he has a variety of voices) and gives a large order, including a number of articles no one is likely to want, which he asks should be packed separately. He mentions, since he is going away, that he would like the order to be delivered to the account address at a certain time the following day, and then meets the van, outside the premises, with the same yarn every time. This is to the effect that, as he is leaving for the country, the vanman should take the unwanted part of the goods to the front door where, he says, the maid will be coming within a few minutes to take them in. The remainder of the goods are then loaded into his car. The vanman (who usually could not care less) is given a £1 with regal generosity, and the car drives away, everyone but the shop being completely satified. There will of course be a few awkward moments for the customer on his return.

Two well-known young criminals, several years ago, were filled with pity at the plight of some families of their acquaintance, who were going to be hard up over Christmas. There was a hasty consultation and the decision was taken that they must be helped. You and I might give of our time and perhaps some of our money to assist in such a case. The underworld does things on an altogether larger scale. Discreet inquiries were made as to the times and habits of the vans that left the food department of one well-known store. A couple of days later, a well-loaded one was neatly hi-jacked from outside the very doors of the emporium and driven away to a more convenient spot. I suppose you might say that they had given of their time and money. A friend of theirs, who told me of the exploit, certainly thought they had behaved most generously. 'Do you know, they only kept the best whisky!' he said. 'There aren't many who would behave like that.' Guiltily aware of often buying presents with which I could not subsequently bear to part, I agreed.

Yes, the underworld likes to keep Christmas in all the old traditional ways. And few things bring home to one the scale on which they live more than the way in which Christmas is kept. You and I go to do our Christmas shopping with some care, with limited time and limited money. Our anxiety is to find the present that will please at a reasonable cost. The underworld's sights are set far higher. They do their shopping also and they have a fine, long Christmas list. But that Christmas list is usually marked off in *Kelly's Directory*. 'Jennifer's Diary' and similar social calendars are also useful possessions. Combined with *Kelly's Directory*, they give a clear indication of the value of parties that will be held, where, and on which dates. Armed thus, the good thief in search of a good Christmas, who also knows the best family jewels, has a fairly shrewd idea of where his shopping can be done. His wife or his bird will have sighed envious sighs at the charity ball where she beheld Lady X wearing jewellery she herself particularly coveted. It is a point of honour, indeed of chivalry, in the underworld, that her man will get it for her for Christmas. There are, in the last resort, of course, the best jewellers to consider; but only the man who is prepared to shop long before Christmas has any real chance of getting coveted presents from this source. A remark brought this home to me the other day. One of my underworld friends, recovering from a Saturday night, was taking a Sunday stroll down Bond Street – it is as well to keep an eye on interesting things even if your liver is playing up. He saw a safe being brought out of a well-known shop. He saw another going in. He drew a little nearer and observed, to his chagrin, that the dear old safe going out was a very defective one indeed. 'Just fancy that', he said with great indignation, 'there was a safe there all those years that you – I mean *you* – could have opened with a nail file! And to think of the chances we have all been missing, reckoning that

that particular shop was guarded to the teeth! It breaks my heart to think what a lot of trouble it would have saved me getting the bird's birthday present.'

With the police squared; with food and drink provided free of charge; and with the possible satisfaction of a year's good work past and the anticipation of a year's good work to come, a criminal family may settle down to a happy Christmas of an almost Dickensian flavour. But not always. Though business is sacred and nothing must be allowed to interfere with it in the ordinary way, many a criminal has an Achilles heel and this heel may sometimes even be in his better nature. There is a villain living in the West End who, in addition to the wife of his bosom and a decorative bird, also owns a couple of elderly pekingese dogs, which are the pride of his heart. Unfortunately, his wife loathes them; the bird cannot exactly be brought to the house as dog-sitter though she would gladly do so, being an animal-lover; and the gentleman in question is afraid to have any domestic help in the house in case a large number of articles are identified, or, even worse, the domestic help might be supplied by law. He loves to travel and had thought of a profitable Christmas in the South of France. He was telling his woes to a friend in a West End casino the other day, during one of those pauses when even the habitual gambler stops to draw breath after unusually heavy losses. 'It's no use', he said, 'my Christmas is finished. Those Pekes require attention, close attention. What with the boy Peke's bronchitis and the girl' – he looked round, because he did not wish ladies to overhear – 'the girl', he continued uneasily, 'being you-know-what about that time, I'm just not going to be able to leave them. I had reckoned on a very happy holiday and I'm just not going to get it. Disgusting, these quarantine regulations. They spoil everyone's happiness.'

I myself am sometimes in the South of France at Christmas. I shall in future look round with interest at the genuinely jewelled ladies around me and wonder whether the care of two little dogs in England may be helping to secure their rubies and diamonds. It was in the same casino where the dog lover was talking that I happened to mention the fact that I liked a Cote d'Azur

Christmas. A glassiness came into the eye of one of the group with whom I was speaking, a contact to whom I had only recently been introduced. 'Yes', I added hastily, 'and of the two accounts that I have with London shops, one has withdrawn my credit and the other has strict instructions to take no orders from me by phone.' The glassy expression faded into a slow smile. 'Well, I hope you have a very happy holiday', he said. 'Judging by that last remark, you deserve it.'

Chapter 17

ALL IS HUMAN

The telephone bell, shrilling in my ear, wakes me. It is just about 1 a.m. and my husband, with a groan, says that it is sure to be for me. It is. Inwardly cursing, like the doctor who wishes that babies would not choose to enter the world in the small hours, I lift the receiver. The voice at the other end is cordial. 'Would you like to come down to see Eddie tomorrow?' it says, without salutation, as is the way of this world. 'What do you mean, tomorrow?' I reply sleepily, 'It's Wednesday now – is it Wednesday or Thursday you're talking about?' There is a pause, whilst I try to identify the voice, so like so many others. I decide that it is Bobbie, since Bobbie has a friend by name Eddie, unknown to me so far except by description.

Bobbie it is. 'Oh', he says, 'are you asleep? I didn't reckon it was that late. You go to bed early!' 'I don't', I say, 'but I do get up early and thought I would turn in by eleven tonight. You've ruined my beauty-sleep. Well, what is all this?' Mirth at the other end. 'You forget we're night-workers' comes over the line accompanied by hearty laughter at the witty crack. 'You're getting too old for beauty-sleep', also adds insult to injury. It transpires in due course that Eddie has exhibited a touching desire to see me. From long experience, I know that this means that the unknown Eddie has something to get out of me; but fair enough: I have not yet visited this particular prison, which is an open one. I want to see it, and so I agree. But since the last time I drove with Bobbie, who is a diligent stoppo-driver (going straight, for the moment), it was a positive ride of death, I stipulate that driving shall be on Fordham, rather than underworld lines.

'Take the Bentley', is the astonishing answer. 'That should suit you.' 'My God!' I say, thoroughly wakened at last, 'is it stolen? I am definitely not driving in a ringed car.' This is an insult. 'Nothing of the sort', Bobbie replies, 'you ought to know me better than that.' The trouble is I do know him better than that; but I conclude that a stolen Bentley would be a bit conspicuous and agree to go.

The result is that a few – far too few – hours later – I am driving south with Bobbie, who enlivens the journey by assessing the possibilities of banks that we pass and explaining how, if I should suddenly have an overwhelming desire to rob one, I should proceed. The factual tone of the story is so compelling that I have almost got into the vaults of one National Westminster, when he announces that we will take refreshment and also buy some luxuries for the allegedly starving Eddie. I keep on wishing that I felt really confident about spare number-plates in the back but it is now too late to say anything.

Eventually we arrive at the prison, where the Bentley is waved in in a manner very pleasing to Bobbie, who says, 'Ah! That's class, you see', and I forbear to suggest that he might be taken for my chauffeur. (I have been told to 'dress properly, not slacks'.) By now, it is clear that Eddie's somewhat simple mind has worked it out that my presence as a visitor will in some way improve his social position with the Governor, who does not know me, does not see me, and will never have the slightest interest in my visit. But I hold my tongue: once more the words 'You cannot beat an idea out of them', echo in my mind; so we shell out the chocs and cigarettes, biscuits and Polo-mints we have brought – only to have them waved away by the ungrateful recipient, who says that he is okay, thank you: it's like the Army only better and he can get what he wants from the canteen.[1]

We then get down to a splendid gossip, of the type generally ascribed to women, assessing the characters and prospects of other prisoners (the visit is an open one and takes place in semi-public) and, since Eddie's stretch is only a short one, the conversation is not saddened by the usual questions about parole prospects or family worries. Eddie, in any case, is happy to be away from his bird. It is clear, however, that Eddie has something private to say to Bobbie – almost certainly to do with loot and its concealment – and, both of them being properly aware that I am not

[1] Remember that this is an *open* prison. Things are not so bright in normal detention.

desirous of knowing anything embarrassing to the 'respectable' (I doubt if they would enlighten me in any case – supposing I took a fancy to 'their' property!), I am passed over to an old pal of Eddie's, who, if a casting director for a medieval film set eyes on him, would exactly fill the bill of 'A Melancholy Wight'.

The M.W. buys me a cup of canteen tea and a chocolate biscuit and asks me for news of the East End. I give such information as I have. What do I think of the prison? he asks. I say that it looks perfectly splendid to me – exactly what prisons ought to be, with proper employment, good surroundings and adequate sanitation. Not to mention absence of *dogs*, regarded with horror and disdain by all right-minded prisoners ('You'd think we was slaves!'). To my surprise, the M.W. looks at me with disgust and tells me I don't know nothing. I do not appreciate the barren monopoly (monotony?) of the open spaces and the lack of routine. The M.W. has served many a stretch and has been sent to this particular nick by a kindly bench who no doubt think that they are doing him a considerable favour. They would be astonished at his reaction. 'Wish I was back at . . .', he says.[2] 'They know how to treat you there. Get a steak and chips any night after lock-up." This extraordinary tribute to a nick usually considered (especially by reformers) to be a disgrace to a civilised country is sorrowful confirmation of the fact that prisoners become institutionalised and yearn for familiar routines and surroundings,[3] sordid though they may be. Nor, on reflection, is this anything new.

My father used at regular intervals to defend a dear old man, known as the Dartmoor Shepherd. His speciality was sacrilege, that is to say, robbing church offertory-boxes which rarely contained more than a few shillings. A more gentle, harmless nutter could hardly be imagined and he regarded Dartmoor, which was then a place of unspeakable horror, as his only home. Everyone there knew and liked him, and when he was released, always with a few shillings and nothing else, he would come to see my

[2] I am sorry not to be able to give the name of this desirable prison, but feel that it would be rather mean.

[3] It is always surprising to me, even after all this time, that prisoners who are used to luxury at home seem to miss it so little. It must be, I think, that the luxury is more a prestige-symbol than liked for itself.

father, who invariably produced a few more shillings and good advice; but sadly knowing that the poor old fellow was lonely and lost and would inevitably break into another church with the sole idea of getting back into Dartmoor. He did once keep out of trouble for a few months, but that was when his sister was alive. After that, there was no one in the world but the warders to be his friends. I remember skipping along beside him on one of his coming-out visits and saying to him with juvenile candour, 'You won't steal from our church, will you? Daddy wouldn't like that'; to get the reply 'You're a very rude little girl and your Daddy wouldn't like that either', which, in retrospect, was both fair and true. He bore me no grudge: for years after that, religious Christmas cards used to arrive from him, the piety of which was only surpassed by an equally regular one from Broadmoor, for my father, from a client who had murdered a number of his family!

The M.W. was interesting to me since he proved that the old attitudes still exist among younger generations of crook. Despite a look of some age – I have commented before on the ageing effects of a criminal life – he is only in his mid-thirties. He is unlikely to reform. This is not surprising. What is really astonishing, in the present state of our penal administration, is that more than a handful of convicted men ever make any effort at all to go straight after experience of English prisons. This should be qualified at once by saying that there *are* prisons (this is one) where genuine attempts are made to provide men with the means to learn an honest trade, to inspire some sort of feeling for justice and respectability and, above all, to bring them into contact with someone who *cares*. C. A. Joyce, who knows more about men in prison than anyone else of my acquaintance and who has taught me what little I know of how to be of help, once said that men reform for a *person*, not an idea, and he is one hundred percent right.

But what chance has the best and most inspired Governor of the majority of our prisons? Home Secretary after Home Secretary makes statements about the increase in crime figures: Press feeds public with horror stories about crime, from details of every sort of violence to complaints, sometimes aimed at the Home Office, sometimes at the underworld, about the overcrowded state of our prisons.

A good Prison Governor gets his heart broken by the conditions in which he is supposed to inspire and reform his charges. Huge Victorian buildings, often today surrounded by a complex of high-rise flats which make security a nightmare, owing to ease of signalling; a shortage of prison-officers which means an intake of unsuitable ones; public demands for security which cannot be met by anything but inhumane conditions[4] – these are only some of the problems which he has to face. There is not nearly enough provision of interesting and tiring work: 'tiring' because a man must use up energy creatively if he is not to channel it into something else, and, if Satan finds some mischief still for idle hands to do, he is even quicker to seize on a combination of idle hands and idle brain. Hard factory-work is a greater reformer than solitary confinement. 'What am I to do?' said one Governor of great integrity to me. 'I've got some of the most explosive boys in any nick and no work to give them which takes up a fraction of their energies.' Petty and niggling restrictions get imposed by Governors bored or worn-out by frustration; tempers become frayed by trifles which mean too much to men whose world has shrunk to minutiae; something sets off the spark which lights a fuse in the packed explosive and there is a riot. The public, naturally, blame the cons.

Sometimes they are right to do so. Mostly, we should blame ourselves for the fact that money to be spent on our prisons is the lowest priority there is. The worse the prisoner, the more it will take to do anything with him. We have got to discover how to reform people in sheer self-defence. I mentioned the Melancholy Wight to one of the high-ups in the Dutch penal administration. The Dutch are tough. So are their criminals. But Dutch prisoners seldom return to gaol. 'This is exactly the problem we faced and I think we have dealt with it. To stop a man becoming prison-minded is one of the most economical things you can do. It takes great care in each case and it means paying attention to every single individual.' There was loud, rude laughter among the

[4] Lord Mountbatten, so often blamed for these, in fact said in his report that they were a disgrace to any civilised country. No one has *hurried* to remove them though they will soon be replaced. By what? The answer varies.

Badger's members to whom I put this story. Individual attention was the last thing *they* wanted. A nick where they knew the ropes and got into a comfortable routine was the idea. Anyway, 'See the screws wanting more of our company! You must be joking!' So I went on to inform them that the careful selection of prison for prisoner was the nucleus of the Dutch system, instead of the higgledy-piggledy-put-him-wherever-there-is-room system which operates perforce (more or less) in this country.

Here, surprisingly, I got some support. Naturally, the prime factor in this was self-interest. 'Joe'd be interested. He was trying hard to get to the Scrubs', said Alf, almost enthusiastically. 'He's heard that there was some special classes there. Bitter disappointed he was – nothing but trouble since.' Joe, if my memory is correct, has a foreign girlfriend at the moment and has been doing language courses in his present nick. He was, when I last saw him, hissing with indignation, having been sold the idea, accurately or otherwise, that the authorities would not transfer him because they thought that his anxiety to get transferred was in order to facilitate escape, a theory which, according to Joe, was assisted by a desire to get fluent in a foreign tongue. This idea of Joe's was probably rubbish: what matters, however, is that these notions get around and are supported. The Home Office may have forgotten what started off the Indian Mutiny: trifles still blow up into thunderstorms and attitudes become fixed. The resentment Joe and most other prisoners feel over appeals to authority and incomprehensible decisions is perfectly understandable. It makes it very difficult to get 'through' to men who are difficult enough already.

At the root of quite ninety per cent of prison difficulties – this is not said carelessly but on reasoned assessment – lies the fact that our prison system, overburdened and tagged on to a department which is a ragbag of oddments that have, like Topsy, 'just growed' is not adapted to dealing with the problems which face such an administration today. Most journalistic colleagues would agree with me that the Home Office is about the most maddeningly inefficient department of all the government offices with which we have to deal. Most journalists are not even as charitable as that, but there is good reason to know what the pressure is on the prison section and, whilst cursing the buck-passing, the lack of anyone who is prepared to see a job through,[5] the constant change of personnel, the lack of liaison and the tendency for any named official to be in Strasbourg, on leave or sick (there seems to be a very high disease-rate amongst them), I know well that I should not like to be in their shoes. Unless, that is, rocket-firing was included in my powers.

One could go on filling books with stories about the Home Office and I have no intention of doing so. I give Joe's story as one small example of a perfectly reasonable request, turned down without any explanation, most probably for a sound and sensible reason. But why not tell it him? No one in prison ever seems to get any reason given for almost every decision taken about him: nor does he know the faceless people who make it. In all probability the real reason for all this is that no one has got time; or it is even more likely that it is just lack of imagination. They are nice people in the Home Office, so nice that it is difficult to imagine them sitting cheek by jowl with the people they 'administrate'; but any familiarity with criminals, such as my own, is there considered subversive though in fact, like many, many others, I work extremely hard to put over the idea that there is a lot to be said for an honest life and that justice really stands for something. Unhappily, any appeal to the underworld on these lines falls flat when justice *seems* to be the faceless men not caring a hang about prisoners' worries (things going wrong at home are common and cause trouble 'inside'), not helping them sufficiently over the requirements for parole or informing them as to why they have been turned down. It is the awful impersonality of Justice which breeds the Melancholy Wight's attitude. This attitude is the one which wastes more money and more human beings than anything in the prison system. To win any respect from the underworld, it is essential to keep your word, not to lie to them and try not to let anyone down, however frankly you may tell them what you think of them. It is seldom that anything at all can be done: they do not blame you for this. You have tried and they are almost always touchingly grateful.

[5] I doubt if any single person is so empowered.

Before looking at a few things that work in other countries and might do something over here, there is one more story which shows the cruel inefficiency of present regulations. If it was unique, I should not use it.

It is a requirement of visits to top-security gaols (what is known as 'A' category prisoners, i.e. those who are considered high escape risks and dangerous to the public), that a visitor shall supply the authorities with photographs and various details, after which he or she may be authorised as a fit person to visit. This, intended to stop crooked pals passing messages or organising breakouts, applies rather ludicrously to Her Majesty's Counsel! Embarassed police, excusing themselves politely, checked that *my* passport photo was a fair likeness. One, meaning it nicely, remarked that it flattered me. This, however, was a matter of dealing with a woman, and a common journalist at that. They were horrified at having to subject my husband – Q.C. and sometimes exercising judicial functions – to what they thought was the ignominy of a police visit. What is even sillier, had he been Counsel representing the prisoner he had been asked to visit at the current time (he had done so on various occasions in the past) he would, it appears, not have had to be identified. What a chance, I remarked, for the sort of impersonation that once happened in the war, when a lecturer (Indian) whom I had despatched to address Wrens on the subject of his country, at a very delicate moment politically, arrived at his destination only to be told that the lecture was over and had been highly subversive! Perhaps 'learned Counsel' will arrive one day with a legal red bag full of gelignite. But back to the story.

Robert Welch, one of the thirty-year sentence men from the Mail Train robbery, is a member of an entirely respectable family, good old London stuff, some of whom are taxi-drivers, itself a guarantee of good character. The family, greatly distressed over the younger brother's fate, have kept close touch with him and are determined to set him up in a small business when he gets parole and generally to rally round and see that he keeps straight. Just the thing, one would think, to be encouraged: something rare and what one dreams of in the case of a man who has not had a bad record before one awful lapse. Family ties, say all the experts, are the most vital link to be kept.

One of the taxi-driving brothers accordingly sent in his form and photographs. After about six weeks a letter from the Governor of Albany asked for a few more details which were sent. More time elapsed and then arrived a letter from Robert, with a Visiting Order for three people. I have myself never received a VO which does not specify the visitor: it seems that this one merely stated the number of visitors which, in the circumstances, may have been a mistake.

Charles Welch, the brother in question, thinking that after all this time things must be all right, therefore set off to the Isle of Wight, with wife (who took her passport but did not really expect to be admitted) and Robert Welch's own wife who had been before. He paid the fares and lost a day's work and, in all, spent about twenty pounds. On arrival at Albany, he was refused admission, only Robert's wife being allowed in. He asked to see the Governor, which he could not do. (Quite likely he was not there). The officer on the gate then rang up someone at the Home Office whilst Charles Welch waited for three-quarters of an hour in the waiting-room. Back came the answer 'No joy. You have been approved but not yet accepted.' By which, one assumes, was meant that the photos had not been sent through. The bitter disappointment can be imagined. Robert Welch is highly-strung and nervous. In conditions of top-security this is just the sort of thing which makes a man have an outburst which jeopardises his good record and counts against remission.[6]

Does this seem a trivial story? Not if you know the world of prison and realise the damage to law and order that this sort of thing does. The fact that a perfectly honest man has been badly treated, either by inadvertence, incompetence or even muddle, is sad; but it is not nearly so harmful as the inevitable result around the nick where cynicism and distrust extend to all who have them in charge. 'Just like them', goes the tale. 'They do it on purpose

[6] I raised this with the Home Office. Polite police called at the Welch home and things are now okay. I also received an 'official' explanation. But no one, at any time or to anybody, suggested 'Sorry, chum!' Such a chance lost, to show a *human* reaction.

to aggravate you.' 'Yes', says another. 'Just aggro. Do you remember when Fred's missus died and head office (thus do they refer to the department) wouldn't let him out even with the law going with him till twenty-four hours after the funeral. Diabolical, it was. He tore the screws up lovely after that and you'll never get him now that he works with a shooter.' Oh yes, these are really things that have been said. Their truth is dubious; I am quite certain that Fred's tragedy if accurately related was entirely unintentional, the much-respected Governor having leaned over backwards to help. What matters is that they are believed. Of course this is written from the wrong side of the law and will be attacked as partisan. But it is not taking sides. It is reporting, as honestly as I know, what is the result of impersonal handling. If we are to do anything at all with the crime figures and save a penny of the money wasted on recidivism, someone has got to use imagination. The criminal is a human being and when he is treated as a number, good money is being thrown after bad by the continuation of many and many a Melancholy Wight. Welch's story is only one simple, trivial example; but because it concerns a truthful and respectable man, it is a better example than the couple of hundred that could be garnered in from prison.

Well, what can be done? First and most important, the whole prison system needs shifting from the dog-licences and aliens and placing under the control of a new and entirely separate Ministry of Justice. Almost every sensible European country has this arrangement and it works. It at least avoids the private conversations that those of us who do manage to penetrate socially the Establishment of either department or parliamentary representatives enjoy when, often over a tongue-loosening glass, one hears such remarks as 'Well, the Minister is not going to have time, what with Northern Ireland and porno – afraid you're on to a very low priority.'

Within such a Ministry, there should be a section with which prisoners could communicate, with named and known officials as is done in Holland and Scandinavia. Secrecy is always a bad thing, breeding suspicion – goodness knows no underworld character needs any encouragement to it – and even a dusty answer does more to dispel it when it comes from Smith the man, than when it is something read from a buff form from no apparent human being. Another side benefit of more direct communication in other countries is a levelling of conditions. In England, *faute-de-mieux,* the Governor is mainly responsible for day-to-day matters and privileges; hence the anxiety of prisoners to get to this nick or that, where it is known that the 'Governor is a gent' and to leave those where it is said that he is 'a right bastard'. Educational facilities, much appreciated, vary geographically too. It is interesting that creature comforts seem to be relatively unimportant, save for complaints of too long periods locked up or too short exercise-time. The 'atmosphere' is what they all criticise and this is dependent upon the Governor. But not in all respects. 'The Governor's okay but he's coshed by the Home Office,' said one disconsolate con, in reference to some difference of opinion between the Governor, who knew him and was prepared to trust him and the Home Office, who were not prepared to take the risk. Again, the Home Office may have been right but it is undesirable that sections of administration can be played off against each other. A centralised administration, with freer access and more open diplomacy would be much more satisfactory.

The main difficulty in this country is parliamentary responsibility. But here we come upon the worst feature of the present system. Someone must be responsible; but with a vulnerable Minister at the head of the department, only too well aware of an electorate which will speedily give him his chips if any major scandal breaks – and major scandals involving escapes of notorious prisoners move the electorate much more than the woes of wronged convicts – it is only natural that caution, which in the end often amounts to simple inertia, prevails. How can a Home Secretary, as human a being as any in the underworld, be expected to put his own and his party's neck at risk over a few 'hoods': how in all fairness can one expect a man wearied (to take one example) by battle and sudden death in Ulster,[7] to turn reforming zeal on to the prison service? It is simply not on. Beneath him, the permanent officials, good men and true but human also, certainly do not wish to jeopardise their steady advancement

[7] This is not directed at any Home Secretary but simply as an example of a Home Secretary who carries a particularly heavy burden.

up the ladder by taking risks. It is much easier to play for safety and, keeping everything as confidential as possible (for which read 'filed away wherever possible') maintain the *status quo* with all their might. I am not being snide: facts of life are facts of life.

The Swedes get round the problem by having a permanent director in charge of all the everyday running of things. They also have a staff who seem to stay in the job more permanently than ours, who are always getting transferred: and the reason is probably better chance of advancement and better pay. But it is all much more in the open there. Prisoners write to the Press and, within reason, the Press have access to the prisoner. An English civil servant to whom I propounded this appeared about to faint at the suggestion. He must be extremely ignorant as to the way in which newspapers are produced. Such freedom here would produce a flood of barrack-room-lawyer-type letters for a week or two, only a minute fraction of which would be worth any publicity at all. News would then find its own level and, barring something extremely juicy, editors would cease to find interest in prison letters. As, under present conditions, every newspaper, crime-reporter and person like myself is deluged, at intervals, with letters easily smuggled out of prison, it seems a pity not to provide a legitimate outlet and take the taste out of it. To return to administration, it is much easier to experiment quietly and to administer an equable, continuous policy if justice is removed from the immediate parliamentary arena. Things only reach the Swedish parliament if something is seriously wrong or if some big question of policy is envisaged. Far from keeping things dark, it opens things up; but policy and politics are kept in their respective places.

It will cost money, though it will increasingly pay off, to cover improvements, and a probation service which does not depend on devoted men and women prepared to take a miserable salary for an exhausting vocation. Devotion, yes: anyone who works with the underworld must be dedicated to achieve anything; but sufficient reward also to provide leisure and refreshment. Criminals are extremely exhausting to deal with. Everyone knows that Victorian prisons have got to come down, not for the sake of the inmates so much as to make it possible for staff to cope and to enable human contacts that cannot be forged in barrack-sized buildings. Above all, what has to be done in all prisons, is to force the pace, to prevent prison inertia and familiarity settling in to recidivism. More factory prisons, where human life is much more normal: more ties with home and no possibility of the exploitation of routine.

That such a policy works is beginning to be seen from those prisons where human contact is possible. Grendon has already made a deep impression even on the Badger's club. 'Treat you like a human being there,' was being said by a released member the other day. He intends to go straight, after various discussions in the new-type nick: he is almost ture to fall again, perhaps only once more if we are lucky; but he now has that sense of shame which is the first step to better things. He doesn't want to let 'the gentleman down'. Again one remembers C. A. Joyce's dictum and I think of one of my real friends who, trusted by Mr Justice Stable after an appalling record and bound over, 'let him down, really ashamed I was. And when I came up before him again and he gave me a stiff stretch, I made up my mind I'd never have to lower my eyes in front of him again – and I never did.' Nearly twenty years have confirmed that resolve. I wonder how much money Mr Justice Stable's personality has saved us with that brand rescued from the burning, in a world where 'all is human'.

For Product Safety Concerns and Information please contact our EU representative GPSR@taylorandfrancis.com
Taylor & Francis Verlag GmbH, Kaufingerstraße 24, 80331 München, Germany

www.ingramcontent.com/pod-product-compliance
Lightning Source LLC
LaVergne TN
LVHW020638300926
849161LV00004B/741
9781041063957